the essentials...

Palace of Westminster & Big Ben ▶ *1* *

Changing of the Guard at Buckingham Palace ▶ *1*

Tower Bridge & London Bridge ▶ *4*

The City ▶ *4*

Tate Britain ▶ *1*

British Museum ▶ *8*

Queen's Walk & Tate Modern ▶ *5*

Hyde Park & Regent's Park ▶ *7* and ▶ *8*

...and our favourites...

Enjoy the lively atmosphere of Covent Garden and Soho ▶ *2*

Take afternoon tea in one of the large hotels ▶ *1*, ▶ *3* and ▶ *7*

* The numbers indicate the sections.

N. Setchfield /age fot

Tower Bridge

Dine in an Indian restaurant on Brick Lane ▶ *4*

Discover a world of **curiosities** at Sir J. Soane's Museum ▶ *3*

Visit **at no charge** the great museums and galleries and admire masterpieces ▶ *1* National Gallery and ▶ *6* V&A

Try "fish and chips" in one of the best addresses in London ▶ *7*

Stroll through one of the legendary **flea markets** ▶ *8* Camden Town and ▶ *9* Portobello Road

Fish and chips

Fotosearch RM /age fotostock

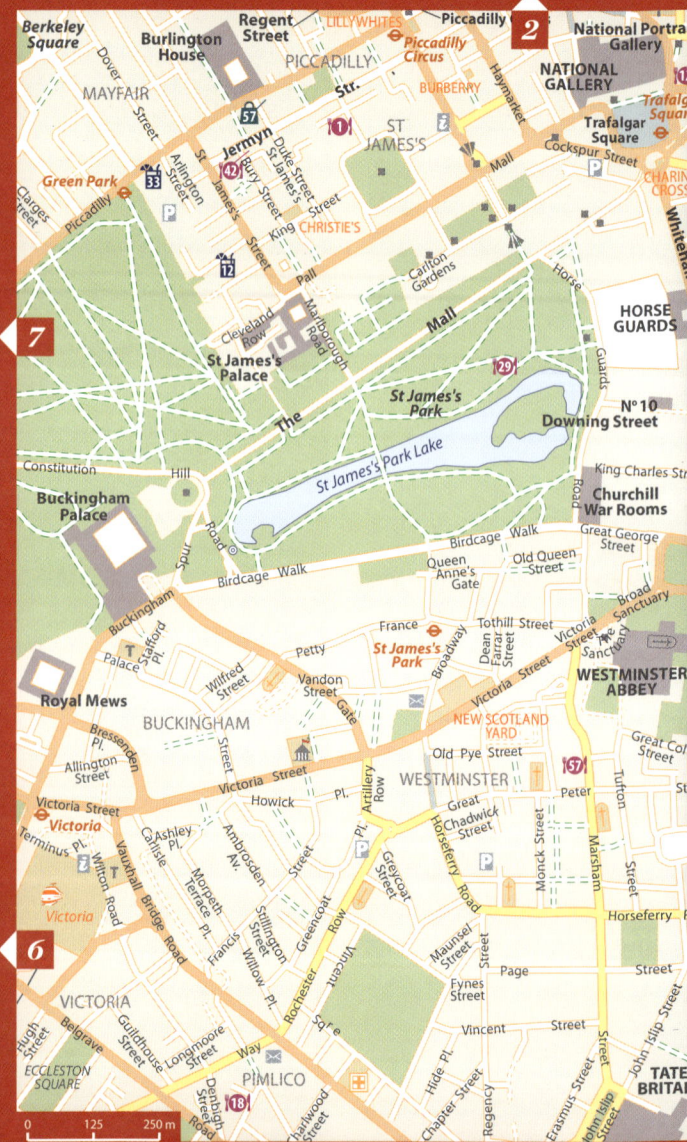

Royal Mews★★ – ⊖ *Victoria -*
www.royalcollection.org.uk - Mar-Oct: 10h-17h
(rest of year: call for details) - £8.50. Since
1825, the royal stables have housed
carriages and official cars used by
the royal family.

WHERE TO EAT

1 Al Duca – *4-5 Duke of York St. -*
⊖ *Piccadilly Circus - ℘ 020 7839 3090 -*
www.alduca-restaurant.co.uk - closed Sun -
dishes £16.50. An Italian restaurant that
offers very good value for money.

12 Café in the Crypt – *Duncannon*
St. - ⊖ *Trafalgar Square - ℘ 020 7766*
1158 - www.stmartin-in-the-fields.org - less
than £15. This self-service café located
in the vaulted crypt of St Martin-
in-the-Fields offers healthy options
and jazz concerts on Wednesday
evenings (after 7pm).

18 Chimes – *26 Churton St. -*
⊖ *Victoria, Pimlico - ℘ 020 7821 7456 -*
www.chimes-of-pimlico.co.uk - dishes £10-15.
Rustic and tasty British cuisine:
let yourself be tempted by the
delicious pies.

29 Inn The Park – ⊖ *St James's Park*
- ℘ 020 7451 9999 - www.innthepark.com -
dishes £13-25. Enjoy good food and
reasonable prices at this restaurant
in the heart of St James's Park.

42 Quaglino's – *16 Bury St. -*
⊖ *Green Park - ℘ 020 7930 6767 -*
www.quaglinos-restaurant.co.uk - closed
Sun - dishes £15-35. People-watch while
enjoying seasonal cuisine at this
watering hole of the well-to-do.

57 The Cinnamon Club –
30-32 Great Smith St. - ⊖ *St James's Park -*
℘ 020 7222 2555 - www.cinnamonclub.com
- closed Sun - dishes £20-35. Delight in
deliciously inventive Indian cuisine in
an exclusive setting.

TAKE A BREAK

Dukes – *St James's Pl. -* ⊖ *Green*
Park. Don't miss the *martini bar* at this
very British hotel — this is where
Ian Fleming was inspired to make
the martini James Bond's the
preferred drink.

22 St Stephen's Tavern – PUB - *10*
Bridge St. - ⊖ *Westminster.* A beautiful
Victorian pub with a cosy atmosphere,
located opposite Big Ben.

33 The Ritz – TEA - *150 Piccadilly -*
⊖ *Green Park - Service every 2h, from 11h30*
to 19h30. Book six weeks in advance,
for this unforgettable experience
(from £47). Dress code.

SHOPPING

⊛ Jermyn Street (⊖ *Piccadilly Circus*).
Original and bespoke shoemakers,
hatters, and tailors for the gentlemen
in your life.

57 Fortnum & Mason – *81 Piccadilly -*
⊖ *Piccadilly Circus. ℘ 020 7734 8040.*
www.fortnumandmason.com. This famous
gourmet paradise founded in 1707
offers a wonderful selection of teas,
biscuits and confectionery, as well
as their legendary luxury hampers.
Get next day delivery UK-wide or
international shipping.

Horse Guards parade

Addresses described in adjoining
sections:
16 53 77 ▶ 3
101 134 96 ▶ 5

Eurasia Press / Photononstop

At the foot of the venerable Big Ben, these magisterial neighbourhoods comprise royal residences, government buildings and world-renowned museums. A visit here is a fine way to discover both royal and democratic Britain.

VISIT

Statue of Boadicea in front of Big Ben

Palace of Westminster★★★ –
⊖ *Westminster - www.parliament.uk/ visiting - guided tours by arrangement - £16.* Shadowed by its famous clock tower (**Big Ben★**), this neo-Gothic palace, a masterpiece of Victorian architecture, has more than 1,000 rooms, 100 staircases and 3km of corridors.

Westminster Abbey★★★ –
⊖ *Westminster - www.westminster-abbey.org - summer: Mon-Fri 9h30-16h30 (Sat 14h30); rest of the year: call for details - £16.* Resting ground of sovereigns and the stage for royal ceremonies, this Gothic abbey impresses with its size and splendid carved decorations.

Tate Britain★★★ – ⊖ *Pimlico - www.tate.org.uk - 10h-18h (Fri 22h).* All major British painters from 1500 to the present under one roof: Blake, Turner, Bacon, Hockney and the rest!

Imperial War Museum★★★ –
⊖ *Lambeth North - www.iwm.org.uk - 10h-18h.* Impressive collections of weapons, uniforms and artifacts from both world wars. The Holocaust exhibit is very moving.

Whitehall★ – ⊖ *Westminster.* Government buildings border this thoroughfare: the entrance to **Downing Street**, where No. 10 houses the prime minister; **Banqueting House★★**, the remains of Whitehall palace; and the barracks of the photogenic **Horse Guards★★★**.

Trafalgar Square★★ – ⊖ *Charing Cross.* At this famous gathering place, **Nelson's column** rises from a pedestal, supported by Landseer's four magnificent bronze lions.

National Gallery★★★ – *Trafalgar Square -* ⊖ *Charing Cross, Leicester Square - www.nationalgallery.org.uk - 10h-18h (Fri 21h).* Enjoy world-class collections of European art.

National Portrait Gallery★★ –
⊖ *Leicester Square, Charing Cross - www.npg.org.uk - 10h-18h (Thu-Fri 21h).* Paintings, sculptures, photos and caricatures reveal the faces of those who forged the history of Britain.

The Mall★★ – ⊖ *Charing Cross.* This beautiful tree-lined avenue is the setting for royal parades.

St James's Park★★ – ⊖ *St James's Park.* Take in views of Buckingham Palace and Whitehall as you stroll through this 23ha royal park.

St James's Palace★★ – ⊖ *Green Park - www.royalcollection.org.uk - closed to the public except for Clarence House: guided visits in Aug: 10h-16h (Sat-Sun 17h30) - £9.50.* Built from 1530-1532 under Henry VIII, this elegant brick mansion has long been (and remains) a royal residence.

Buckingham Palace★★ –
⊖ *Victoria - www.royalcollection.org.uk - Aug-Sep: 9h30-19h30 - £19.50.* Visit late Jul-late Sep. The changing of the guard takes place at 11:30h, rain or shine!

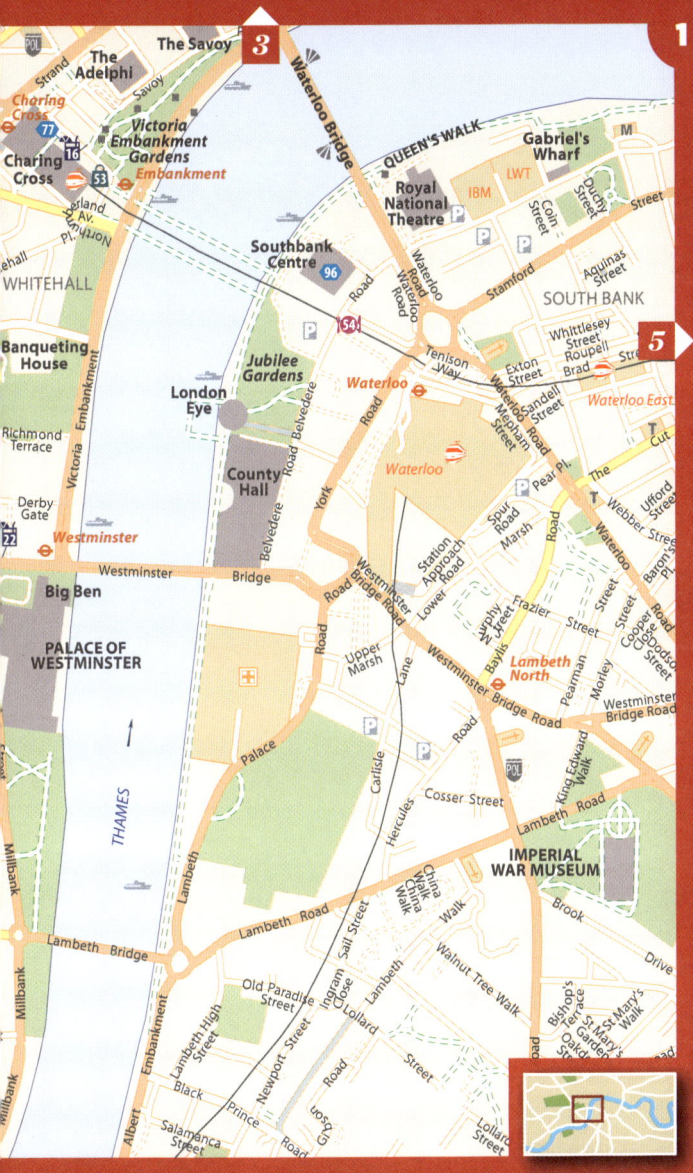

The Savoy
The Adelphi
Strand
Savoy

3

Waterloo Bridge

Charing Cross
77
16
Charing Cross
53
Embankment

Victoria Embankment Gardens
Embankment

QUEEN'S WALK

Gabriel's Wharf
M

LWT
IBM

Coin Street
Duchy Street

Royal National Theatre
P

Southbank Centre
96

Stamford Street

Aquinas Street

SOUTH BANK

WHITEHALL

Northumberland Av.
Cleveland Row

54

Whittlesey Street
Roupell
Brad
Stre

Waterloo Road
Waterloo Road

Tenison Way

Exton Street

Banqueting House

Jubilee Gardens

Waterloo

5

Richmond Terrace

London Eye

Belvedere Road

Waterloo Road

Mepham Street
Scandell Street

Waterloo East

The Cut

Waterloo

Derby Gate

County Hall

York Road

Station Approach

Pear Pl.

Spur Road

Webber Street

Ufford Street

22

Westminster

Westminster Bridge

Belvedere Road

York Road

Westminster Bridge Road
Lower Road

Marsh

Frazier Street
Murphy Street

Waterloo Road

Cooper Road
Baron's Pl.
Doodson Street

Big Ben

PALACE OF WESTMINSTER

Upper Marsh

Baylis Road

Lambeth North

Pearman Street
Morley

Westminster Bridge Road

Carlisle Lane
Hercules Road

Westminster Bridge Road

P

King Edward Walk

THAMES

Cosser Street

Lambeth Road

IMPERIAL WAR MUSEUM

Palace

China Walk
China Walk

Brook

Drive

Lambeth Road

Lambeth Bridge

Sail Street

Walk

Walnut Tree Walk

Millbank

Old Paradise Street

Newport Street
Ingram Close
Lollard Street
Lambeth Walk

Street

Bishop's Terrace
St Mary's Walk
St Mary's Gardens
Oakdene

Lambeth High Street

Albert Embankment

Black Prince Road

Salamanca Street

Gibson Road

Lollard Street

68 **Neal's Yard Remedy** – *17 Shorts Gardens* - ⊖ *Covent Garden*. The flagship store of the organic cosmetics pioneer offers a therapy room for pampering massages, aromatherapy and more.

77 **The Tea House** – *15 Neal St.* - ⊖ *Covent Garden*. Tea lovers will find an extensive selection of black and green teas, both loose and in bags.

78 **Top Shop** – *216 Oxford St.* - ⊖ *Oxford Circus - closed Sun*. The most popular of London's ready-to-wear stores. A must for the fashionista!

79 **VinMag** – *39-43 Brewer St.* - ⊖ *Piccadilly Circus*. A shop specialising in old magazines, old comics, fashion and film magazines.

NIGHTLIFE

71 **100 Club** – *100 Oxford St.* - ⊖ *Oxford Circus, Tottenham Court Road* - *www.the100club.co.uk*. The basement of this iconic club, which saw the birth of punk with the Sex Pistols as well as the mod stylings of The Who and The Kinks in the '60s, today hosts live acts that range from modern jazz to blues and swing.

72 **Bar Rumba** – *36 Shaftesbury Ave.* - ⊖ *Piccadilly Circus*. One of the most popular clubs in London, you can take salsa lessons here.

85 **Ronnie Scott's** – *47 Frith St.* - ⊖ *Leicester Square - réserv.* ☏ *020 7439 0747 - www.ronniescotts.co.uk*. This legendary jazz club continues to offer up great music and atmosphere. Reservations are recommended.

Addresses described in adjoining sections:
101 **102** **124** **33** **57** ▶ *1*
145 **16** **20** **55** **77** ▶ *3*
124 **147** ▶ *8*

G. Azumendi /age fotostock

7

9 Busaba Eathai – *106-110 Wardour St. -* ⊖ *Piccadilly Circus, Tottenham Court Road -* 📞 *020 7255 8686 - www.busaba.com - dishes around £10.* A good place to eat Thai in a casual atmosphere; prepare to queue as reservations aren't accepted.

16 Carom at Meza – *100 Wardour St.-* ⊖ *Piccadilly Circus, Tottenham Court Road -* 📞 *020 7314 4002 - www.caromsoho.com - closed lunchtime and Sun - dishes around £10.* This member of the Conran restaurant group celebrates India just as stylishly and fashionably as its sisters.

51 Ten Ten Tei – *56 Brewer St. -* ⊖ *Piccadilly Circus -* 📞 *020 7287 1738 - closed Sun lunch - dishes at lunchtime around £10, rising to £20 in the evening.* Select from a variety of fresh and Japanese dishes in generous portions and reasonably priced.

TAKE A BREAK

1 Argyll Arms – **PUB** - *18 Argyll St. -* ⊖ *Oxford Circus.* The location explains why this is bustling at all hours, but this historic pub (1716) is worth a visit just to appreciate its original decor.

18 Lamb & Flag – **PUB** - *33 Rose St. -* ⊖ *Covent Garden.* Nestled in a narrow alley, the oldest tavern in the neighbourhood (1623) continues to attract crowds with a cosy and friendly atmosphere and a good selection of beers.

27 The Globe – **PUB** - *37 Bow St. -* ⊖ *Covent Garden.* Opened in 1682, this is one of eight historic pubs on Bow Street, just moments away from the Piazza and opposite the Royal Opera House; popular with tourists and office workers alike.

34 The Salisbury – **PUB** - *90 St Martin's Lane -* ⊖ *Leicester Square.* Built in 1892, the Salisbury is one of the best preserved pubs in London. Be sure to stop off in the afternoon for tea and scones.

SHOPPING

Carnaby Street (⊖ *Oxford Circus*) is home to an array of shops, and you will also find restaurants, trendy bars and clubs.

Berwick Street (⊖ *Piccadilly Circus*) is known for its market and a variety of shopping. At 26 and 30 is the famous Reckless Records **37**.

59 Gerry's – *74 Old Compton St. -* ⊖ *Leicester Square.* From traditional whisky to the rarest absinthe, you're sure to find a measure of happiness in this wine and spirits shop.

62 Hamley's – *188-196 Regent St. -* ⊖ *Oxford Circus.* The world's largest toy store spans six levels and within it you'll find something for all ages.

85 Jubilee Market – *1 Tavistock St. -* ⊖ *Covent Garden.* Vendors rotate through the stalls of this market selling antiques (Mon), miscellaneous goods (Tue-Fri) and handicrafts (Sat-Sun).

66 Liberty & Co – *210-220 Regent St. -* ⊖ *Oxford Circus.* Founded by Arthur Liberty in 1875, this store (in particular, the oldest part on Marlborough St.) merits your attention. On the 3rd floor check out the celebrity portraits made from floral prints.

The beating heart of the city: by day tourists swarm around the innumerable boutiques here. By evening, Soho and Covent Garden become a playground for those enjoying the theatres, pubs, restaurants and clubs.

VISIT

The Piazza★★ - ⊖ *Covent Garden.* This lively square was once the home of a flower market, founded in the 16C. Today, boutiques, coffee shops, cafés and restaurants occupy the old warehouses, designed in 1832 by Charles Fowler and linked by glass walls in 1872. Impromptu music recitals are an entertaining feature at weekends.

London Transport Museum★ - *The Piazza -* ⊖ *Covent Garden - www.ltmuseum.co.uk - 10h-18h - closed Sat - £15.* The exhibits here trace 200 years of London transport network history.

Royal Opera House★ - *Bow Street -* ⊖ *Covent Garden - www.roh.org.uk - guided tour 16h (by appointment) - closed Sun - £9.50.* Built from 1856-1858, this building houses an auditorium of over 2,200 seats and hosts the Royal Opera, the Royal Ballet and the Royal Orchestra.

Chinatown★ - ⊖ *Leicester Square.* Guarded by large oriental porticos, Gerrard Street is the centre of this colourful neighbourhood, which is striking for its exotic character and at its exhilarating best after dark.

Piccadilly Circus★ - ⊖ *Piccadilly Circus.* Located at the end of Piccadilly Street★ Separating Mayfair from St James's, this famous crossroads is one of the nerve centres of London.

Burlington House★ - ⊖ *Piccadilly Circus - www.royalacademy.org.uk - 10h-18h (Fri 22h) - admission charges vary according to the exhibition.* Combining neo-Renaissance and neo-Gothic styles, this building is home to the Royal Academy of Arts, which organises exhibitions and supports contemporary art generally.

Golden Square - ⊖ *Piccadilly Circus.* This quiet, beautiful square with its private garden is the preserve of fashion and media notables.

Regent Street★★ - ⊖ *Oxford Circus, Piccadilly Circus.* This elegant street is renowned for its shops(⟳ *Shopping*), including: the department store **Liberty & Co★★** *(No. 210-220),* the toy store **Hamley's** *(No. 188-196),* and men's fashion emporium **Austin Reed** *(No. 100).* At No. 68 is the luxurious Café Royal.

WHERE TO EAT

🍴**③ Battersea Pie Station -** *28 The Market Building, Lower Ground Floor, Covent Garden -* 📞 *020 7240 9566. www.batterseapiestation.co.uk. Open from 11h daily.* Under the arches of the market building, this eatery serves proper British grub; look for 'The Pie Shop' sign, and pick your pie from an extensive range.

🍴**⑤ Barrafina -** *54 Frith St. -* ⊖ *Leicester Square, Piccadilly Circus -* 📞 *020 7813 8016 - www.barrafina.co.uk - dishes around £10.* Enjoy tapas and a wide selection of Spanish wines. Check out the daily lunchtime specials.

⊖ Goodge St

8

⊖ 24

Store Street

South Crescent

Keppel Street

Malet Street

Montague Place

Bedford Square

Bedford Sq

Bedford Avenue

Windmill Street

Percy Street

Percy Mews

Gresse Street

Stephen Mews

Rathbone Place

Tottenham Court Road

Montague Street

BRITISH MUSEUM

Bedford Place

Bloomsbury Square Gardens

Southampton Row

Vernon Pl

Pitman Pl Row

Bloomsbury Street

Bury Place

Russell

47

Gilbert Pl

Adeline Pl

Great

Bainbridge Street

Dyott Street

New Oxford Street

Museum Street

West Central Street

Streatham Street

New Oxford Street

⊖ Tottenham Court Rd

Hanway Pl

Perry's Pl

Oxford Street

Oxford Street

Bucknall Street

Shaftesbury Avenue

Central Street

Holborn

New Oxford Street

High

20

Newton Street

Stukeley Street

Macklin Street

Wild Street

Sheraton Street

Soho Square

House of St Barnabas

Denman Street

Denmark Street

New Compton Street

Stacey Street

Endell Street

Gardens

Betterton Street

Dury

Arne Street

Dean Street

Frith Street

Greek Street

SOHO

Bateman Street

Charing Cross Road

Mercer Street

68

Monmouth Street

Shorts Gardens

COVENT GARDEN

9
16

Meard Street

5

85

Old Compton St

Tower Street

Shelton Street

West Street

77

Covent Garden

Royal Opera House

Bow Street

27

3

59

Wardour Street

Dansey Pl

Gerrard Street

CHINATOWN

Long Acre

Floral Street

Covent Garden Market

Piazza

Theatre Royal Drury Lane

London's Transport Museum

79

Archer Street

Brewer Street

Shaftesbury Av.

72

Lisle Street

Leicester Pl

Leicester Square

Bear Street

New Row

Bedfordbury

St Paul's Church

18

3

Exeter Street

85

Jubilee Market

Coventry Street

⊖ Piccadilly Circus

Piccadilly Circus

LILLYWHITES

Piccadilly Circus

BURBERRY

Panton Street

Orange Street

Leicester Square

34

St Martin's Lane

Charing Cross Road

Chandos Pl

Agar Street

Bedford Street

45
35

The Savoy

Regent St

ST JAMES'S

Charles II Street

Haymarket

Pall Mall East

National Portrait Gallery

NATIONAL GALLERY

Trafalgar Square

NELSON'S COLUMN

12

Duncannon Street

Charing Cross

Strand

Strand

⊖ Charing Cross

77

16

Buckingham Street

The Adelphi

Victoria Embankment Gardens

Charles II Street

Pall Mall

Warwick House Street

Waterloo Pl

Carlton Gardens

The Mall

⊖ CHARING CROSS

Trafalgar Square

Northumberland Av

Whitehall

Whitehall Pl

1

20 **Princess Louise** – PUB - *208 High Holborn* - ⊖ *Holborn*. This superb late 19C pub, named in honour of the fourth daughter of Queen Victoria, is worth visiting for its beautiful Victorian decor.

35 **The Savoy** – TEA - *The Strand* - ⊖ *Charing Cross, Covent Garden* - ℘ *020 7235 2000 - 10h-20h at the Savoy Tea, 13h30-17h45 in the Thames Foyer*. Jacket required for men. It's an indulgence, but the unique experience makes tea at the Savoy worth the expense. Reservations are required.

SHOPPING

53 **Charing Cross Collectors Fair** – *Villiers St.* - ⊖ *Embankment - Sat 8h30-17h*. Located in the underground station, this market features coins, stamps, medals and badges.

67 **London Silver Vaults** – *53 Chancery Lane* - ⊖ *Chancery Lane - closed Sat afternoon and Sun*. Some 40 shops assembled underground and defended by an armoured door offer beautiful silver objects in a variety of styles ranging from Georgian to modern.

74 **R Twining & Co** – *216 The Strand* - ⊖ *Temple*. The famous tea sellers have had a shop here since 1706. Peruse the wide selection of teas and visit the museum tracing the history of the house.

NIGHTLIFE

77 **Heaven** – *The Arches, Villiers St.* - ⊖ *Charing Cross - closed Tue, Wed and Sun*. A gay paradise with three dance floors featuring different styles from techno to disco. Arrive early: the place is often crowded.

Addresses described in section 2:
18 **27** **77** **85**

Photoshot/hemis.fr

St Mary-le-Strand – *184A Fleet St. - ⊖ Temple - Tue-Thu 11h-16h, Sun 10h-13h.* Built in a Baroque style (1714-1728), this place of worship is known as "the Church of the Taxi Drivers".

Somerset House★★ – *Access by the Strand and Victoria Embankment - ⊖ Temple - www.somersethouse.org.uk - guided visit, no charge, Thu and Sat.* This magnificent late-18C building is home to the **Courtauld Gallery★★** (*www.courtauld.ac.uk - 10h-18h - £5*), best known for its collection of impressionist paintings.

The Savoy – *⊖ Charing Cross.* Decorated in typical British style, the Savoy Hotel is one of the most famous of London.

The Adelphi – *⊖ Charing Cross, Embankment.* This small district falls between the Strand and the River Thames, from Villiers Street to Adam Street. During the 18C and 19C, the area fancied itself as a kind of small Athens, having gained the favour of artists.

Victoria Embankment Gardens★ – *⊖ Embankment.* On the north side of the Thames, these gardens created in 1864 serve as a venue for concerts in summer.

Charing Cross Station – *⊖ Charing Cross.* Built in 1863, this station serves southern England. The neo-Gothic station hotel (1864) and surrounding buildings dating back to 1990 are worth a look.

Ice rink in front of Somerset House

WHERE TO EAT

8 Bleeding Heart Restaurant & Bistro – *Bleeding Heart Yard (access by Greville St.) - ⊖ Farringdon - ℘ 020 7242 8238 - www.bleedingheart.co.uk - closed Sat-Sun - dishes £12-25.* This French establishment located in a discrete courtyard offers three different restaurants to satisfy all budgets.

45 Simpson's-in-the-Strand – *100 The Strand - ⊖ Charing Cross - ℘ 020 7836 9112 - www.simpsonsinthestrand.co.uk - dishes £19-35.* Famous for its roasted meats, Simpson's has been a popular feature on the Strand since 1828.

64 The White Swan – *108 Fetter Lane - ⊖ Chancery Lane - ℘ 020 7242 9696 - www.thewhiteswanlondon.com - closed Sat-Sun - dishes £15-24.* Set in a refined dining room above a cosy pub nearby Fleet Street, it's a safe bet for great food.

65 Tom's Kitchen – *Somerset House - ⊖ Charing Cross - ℘ 020 7845 4646 - www.tomskitchen.co.uk - closed Sun eve - dishes £13-30.* In this elegant and well-restored Georgian house, the menu is composed exclusively of British produce. Don't skimp on dessert!

TAKE A BREAK

10 Cittie of Yorke – PUB - *22 High Holborn - ⊖ Chancery Lane. Closed Sun.* This pub, founded in 1667 and today a Grade II Listed Building, is a marvel: a deep cathedral nave, a confessional and above all, a bar wherein to find refuge! Dylan Thomas wrote an impromptu ode to the pub when it was Henekey's Long Bar.

16 Gordon's Wine Bar – PUB - *47 Villiers St. - ⊖ Embankment.* Serving wine since 1364, Gordon's now offers a wide selection of cheeses to go with it.

Calmer and distanced from the crowds, these neighbourhoods have many advantages: beautiful architecture, a legacy from their aristocratic and legal past; pretty green spaces, and many venues to keep yourself entertained.

Sir John Soane's Museum

VISIT

Gray's Inn★ - *8 South Square -* ⊖ *Chancery Lane.* An illustrious law school whose buildings date back to the 16C.

Sir John Soane's Museum★★ - *13 Lincoln's Inn Fields -* ⊖ *Holborn - www.soane.org - Tue-Sat 10h-17h.* This museum was designed by the architect John Soane at the turn of the 19C with the aim of bringing his art and archaeology collections to the public.

Lincoln's Inn★★ - ⊖ *Chancery Lane - www.lincolnsinn.org.uk - park and chapel closed at weekends.* The site belonged to the Dominicans until 1276, when it was acquired by the Earl of Lincoln whose large house became a residence for law students.

Lincoln's Inn Fields - ⊖ *Holborn.* Palladian-style *(Nos. 57 and 58)* and Georgian *(Nos. 5 and 9) homes* frame this cosy space.

Staple Inn★ - ⊖ *Chancery Lane.* Law students spent their first year in this school of the Chancery. With its Tudor-style wood slats, the Holborn façade (1586-1596) provides a glimpse of medieval London.

High Holborn - ⊖ *Chancery Lane.* Intellectual and cultural traditions are preserved on this avenue in the shape of prestigious institutions such as the Prudential Assurance Building (late 19C-early 20C) with its massive, red edifice at Nos. 138-142.

Fleet Street - ⊖ *Temple, Blackfriars.* For years a stomping ground of journalists, this main thoroughfare and royal road is lined with imposing buildings in a variety of architectural styles.

St Bride's★ - *Fleet St. -* ⊖ *Blackfriars - closed Sat.* A distinctive presence on the London skyline, this church is known for its white spire (69m high) pierced with large open windows; it is the second tallest of Wren's churches.

Temple★ - *Access by Inner Temple Gateway (between Nos. 16 and 17 Fleet St.).* Here lies an amazing labyrinth of courtyards, arches, passageways and gardens leading down to the banks of the Thames. Dedicated to the judiciary, this place offers a haven of quiet amid 17C and 18C buildings.

Lloyd's Law Courts Branch - *222 Strand -* ⊖ *Temple.* This former tavern served as the restaurant for the Courts from 1883 and since 1895 has housed a branch of Lloyds bank.

Royal Courts of Justice - ⊖ *Temple.* The Royal Courts building was built in the Perpendicular style between 1874 and 1882.

St Clement Danes★ - *St Clement Danes Church Strand -* ⊖ *Temple.* Destroyed by fire in 1941, the church was restored in 1982 by the Royal Air Force and served as its sanctuary.

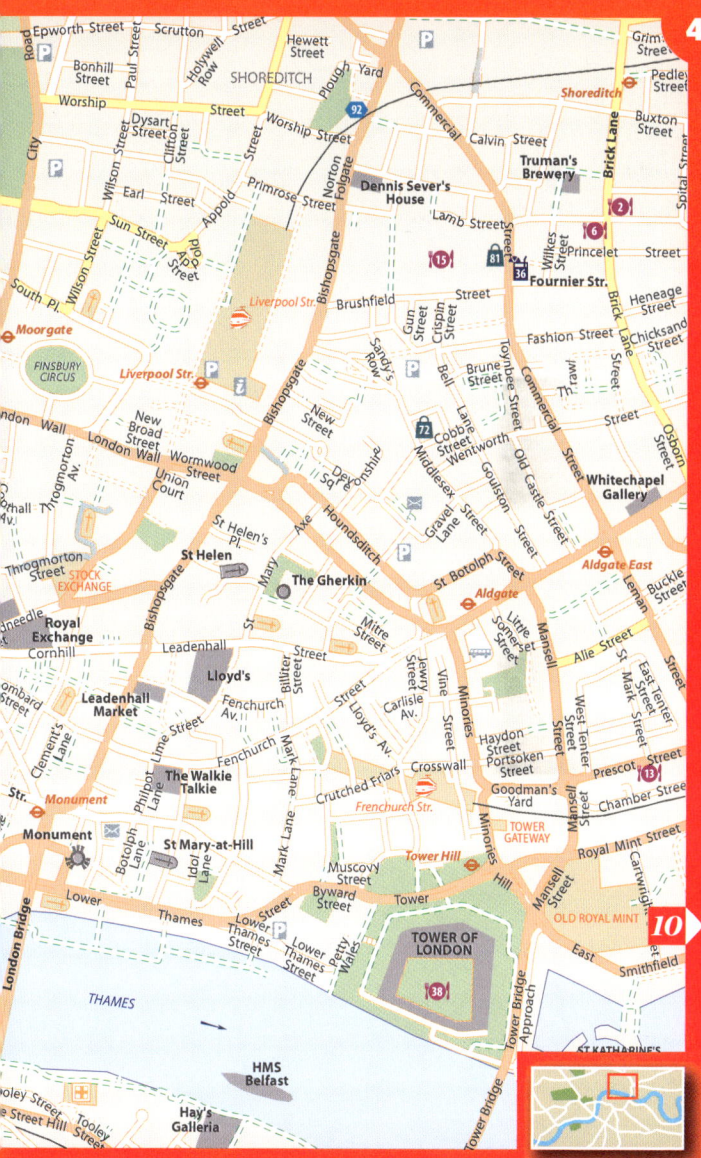

4

Epworth Street · Scrutton · Street · Hewitt Street
Bonhill Street · Paul Street · Holywell Row · Plough Yard
Worship · SHOREDITCH · Commercial · Shoreditch
Pedley Street
Road · City · Dysart Street · Clifton Street · Worship Street · Norton Folgate · Calvin Street · Buxton Street
Bonhill Street · Grimsby Street

92

Wilson Street · Earl · Street · Appold · Primrose · Bishopsgate · Brick Lane · Spital Street

Truman's Brewery

2
6
Princelet · Street

Dennis Sever's House

Lamb Street · Wilkes Street · Heneage Street

South Pl. · Sun Street · Wilson Street

15
81
36
Fournier Str.

Moorgate · Liverpool St. · Brushfield · Street · Crispin Street · Fashion Street · Chicksand Street · Osborn Street

FINSBURY CIRCUS

Liverpool Str. · Sandy's Row · Gun Street · Bell · Brune Street · Toynbee Street · Commercial · Thrawl · Street

New Broad Street · New Street · Cobb Street · Wentworth · Old Castle Street · Whitechapel Gallery

London Wall · Wormwood Street · Union Court · Devonshire Sq · Middlesex · Goulston Street

72

Throgmorton Av. · Cornhall Av. · St Helen's Pl. · Houndsditch · Gravel Lane · Street

St Helen · St Mary Axe · Carlisle Av. · St Botolph street · Aldgate East · Buckle · Leman

STOCK EXCHANGE

The Gherkin · St Botolph street · Aldgate · Little Somerset Street · Alie Street · East Tenter · West Tenter · Mansell · Maik St.

Needle · Royal Exchange · Cornhill · Leadenhall · Mitre Street · Jewry Street · Vine · Minories · Prescot Street

13

Lombard Street · Lloyd's · Billiter Street · Carlisle Av. · Haydon Street · Portsoken Street · Chamber Stree

Leadenhall Market · Fenchurch Av. · Lloyd's Av. · Crosswall · Goodman's Yard

Clement's Lane · Lime Street · Fenchurch · Mark Lane · Crutched Friars · Fenchurch Str. · TOWER GATEWAY

The Walkie Talkie · Philpot Lane · St Mary-at-Hill · Muscovy Street · Byward Street · Tower Hill

Monument · Botolph Lane · Idol Lane · Tower · Hill · Mansell Street · Royal Mint Street · Cartwright

OLD ROYAL MINT

10

London Bridge · Lower · Thames · Street · Petty Wales · TOWER OF LONDON · Tower Bridge Approach · Smithfield

38

THAMES

ST KATHARINE'S

HMS Belfast · Tooley Street · Street Hill · Hay's Galleria

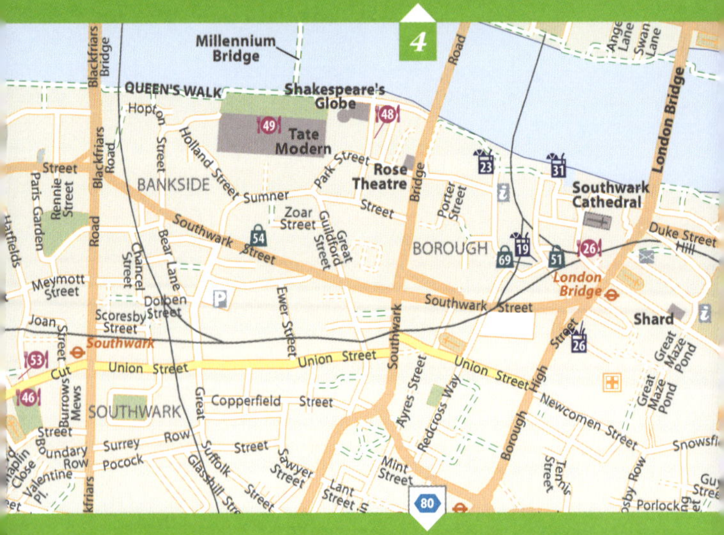

Millennium Bridge

QUEEN'S WALK

Shakespeare's Globe

Hopton Street

Blackfriars Bridge

49 Tate Modern

48

BANKSIDE

Holland Street

Park Street

Rose Theatre

Southwark Cathedral

23

31

Blackfriars Road

Sumner Street

Zoar Street

Great Guildford Street

Porter Street

Paris Garden

Rennie Street

Blackfriars Street

Bear Lane

54

BOROUGH

19 **51** **26**

Rose Street

London Bridge

Meymott Street

Chancel Street

Dolben Street

69

Duke Street Hill

Joan Street

Scoresby Street

Southwark Street

Shard

Southwark

53

Ewer Street

Union Street

Union Street

Union Street

Southwark Street

Newcomen Street

26

46

Cut

Burrows Mews

SOUTHWARK

Copperfield Street

Ayres Street

Redcross Way

Borough High Street

Great Maze Pond

Snowsfi

Surrey Row

Pocock Street

Great Suffolk Street

Sawyer Street

Lant Street

Mint Street

Tennis Street

Crosby Row

Guy

Porlock

80

---

54 **The Archduke** – *Concert Hall Approach* - ⊖ *Waterloo* - ☏ *020 7928 9370* - *www.blackandbluerestaurants.com* - *dishes £10-35*. Arranged under the arches of the railway line, this friendly restaurant specializes in grilled meats. In the evenings, you can hear live jazz performances.

TAKE A BREAK

☕ There are many cafés and cultural institutions along Queen's Walk.

19 **Monmouth** – *2 Park St.* - ⊖ *London Bridge - closed Sun*. Delicious coffee aromas waft out of this little shop where coffee fiends can partake, or buy some to brew at home.

26 **George Inn** – **PUB** - *77 Borough High St.* - ⊖ *London Bridge*. Beams and galleries set the scene at this pub that's straight out of the 17C. In summer, the courtyard hosts Shakespeare plays.

Café in Borough Market

23 **The Anchor** – **PUB** - *34 Park St.* - ⊖ *London Bridge*. This historic pub is situated at the foot of Southwark Bridge. Inside is a maze of small, dark rooms. There's also a beautiful terrace overlooking the Thames.

31 **The Old Thameside Inn** – **PUB** - *Pickfords Wharf, 2 Clink St.* - ⊖ *London Bridge*. Ideal for enjoying a pint while watching the traffic on the Thames. From the terrace, the view of the replica of the *Golden Hinde* ship is outstanding.

curves (2002) was designed by Norman Foster.

Tower Bridge★★ – ⊖ *Tower Hill, London Bridge - exhibition: Apr-Sep 10h-18h; Oct-Mar 9h30-17h30 - £8.* Flanked by iconic neo-Gothic towers, this drawbridge is known worldwide. The pedestrian walkway offers breathtaking views of the city.

Butler's Wharf – ⊖ *Tower Hill, London Bridge.* Luxury apartments, cafés and restaurants have taken over this set of brick warehouses, renovated in the 1980s.

WHERE TO EAT

Gabriel's Wharf (*56 Upper Ground - ⊖ Waterloo*) is lined with cafés and restaurants with pleasant terraces perfect for waterfront snacking.

26 Fish! – *Cathedral St., Borough Market - ⊖ London Bridge - ℘ 020 7407 3803 - www.fishkitchen.com - dishes £12-30.* At the heart of Borough Market, this place lives up to its name, serving fish, grilled or steamed.

48 Tas Pide – *20-22 New Globe Walk - ⊖ London Bridge - ℘ 020 7928 3300 - www.tasrestaurant.com - dishes £9-13.* In front of the Globe Theatre and behind a façade covered with flowers, this restaurant serves tasty Turkish cuisine in generous portions. Another address: *33 The Cut - ⊖ Southwark - ℘ 020 7928 2111*.

49 Tate Modern Restaurant – *℘ 020 7887 8888 - www.tate.org.uk - closed evenings except Fri-Sat - dishes £15-25.* On Level 6 at the Tate, this restaurant offers one of the best views of London, as well as an exceptional wine list.

53 The Anchor & Hope – *36 The Cut - ⊖ Southwark - ℘ 020 7928 9898 - www.anchorandhopepub.co.uk - closed Sun evenings - dishes £15-20.* One of the best gastropubs in all of London, serving original dishes that draw from both English and French traditions.

On the right bank of the Thames, Queen's Walk is a long promenade that stretches from Westminster Bridge to Southwark. Following extensive redevelopment, this former fisherman's district is now well established as a cultural and tourist attraction.

VISIT

London Eye

London Eye★ – ⊖ *Waterloo - adult prices from £19.35.* This Ferris wheel makes a spectacular landmark on the banks of the Thames, offering riders expansive views of up to 20km.

Jubilee Gardens – ⊖ *Waterloo.* Popular place with Londoners, this green space, commemorates the 25-year reign of Queen Elizabeth II.

Southbank Centre★ – *Belvedere Rd -* ⊖ *Waterloo - www.southbankcentre. co.uk.* A stark example of the Brutalist architecture of the 1970s, this building is home to the most famous cultural complex in London (♪ *Nightlife*).

Waterloo Bridge – The architect GG Scott conceived this arched bridge in 1945. A used-book market stands on the banks beneath the bridge.

Royal National Theatre★★ – ⊖ *Waterloo - www.nationaltheatre.org.uk.* Architect Denys Lasdun united three theatres in this space, where some 300 actors with up to 500 costumes put on 20 shows per year.

Gabriel's Wharf – *56 Upper Ground -* ⊖ *Waterloo.* The wharf is home to a number of craft shops and cafés set around a pleasant courtyard.

Tate Modern★★ – ⊖ *Southwark - www.tate.org.uk - 10h-18h (Fri-Sat 22h).* This former power plant, erected in 1960 on the banks of the river and crowned with a glass superstructure, has become one of the world's temples of contemporary art.

Millenium Bridge – Designed by Norman Foster, this steel suspension bridge for pedestrians is a real feat of engineering and architecture.

Shakespeare's Globe★★ – *21 New Globe Walk -* ⊖ *London Bridge - www.shakespearesglobe.com - 9h-17h30 - £13.50.* This replica of the Globe Theatre (16C) is dedicated to the cult of Shakespeare. Some plays are performed outdoors in the afternoon and without artificial lighting (*Apr-Oct*), as they were in the Bard's lifetime.

Rose Theatre – *56 Park St. -* ⊖ *London Bridge - www.rosetheatre. org.uk - Sat 10h-17h.* Part of this 1587 foundation of this 1587 theatre was rediscovered in 1989.

Southwark Cathedral★★ – ⊖ *London Bridge.* This is the oldest Gothic sanctuary in England.

HMS Belfast – ⊖ *London Bridge - 10h-16h - £17.50.* Anchored upstream of Tower Bridge since 1971, this 11,500-ton cruiser distinguished itself during the 1944 Normandy landings.

Hay's Galleria – *Tooley St. -* ⊖ *London Bridge.* Opposite London Bridge Station, this old warehouse is home to elegant shops and cafés.

City Hall – ⊖ *London Bridge - 8h30-18h (Fri 17h30), closed Sat-Sun.* Home to London's mayor, this unique, some would say bizarre, building with glass

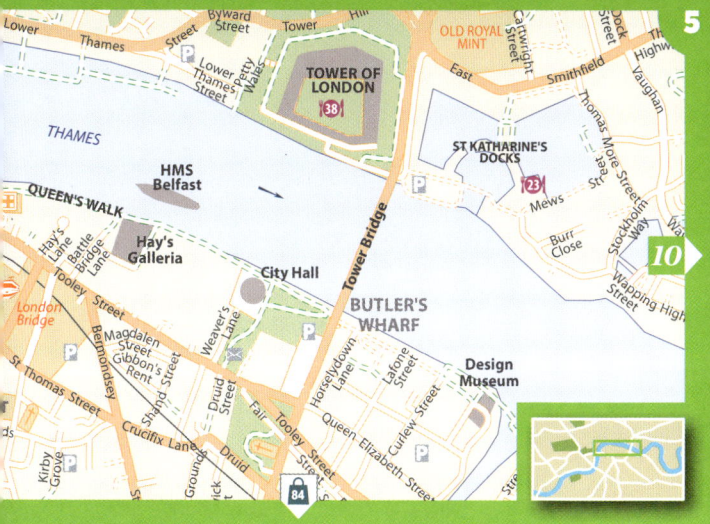

SHOPPING

84 **Bermondsey Market** – *Not on map, corner of Bermondsey St. and Long Lane -* ⊖ *London Bridge - Fri 6h-14h.* This antique market is a delight for collectors of jewellery, cutlery or crockery, especially in silver.

51 **Borough Market** – *8 Southwark St. -* ⊖ *London Bridge - Wed-Sat.* The oldest food market in London focuses on organic foodstuffs and fine or rustic specialities of England and the continent.

54 **Contemporary Applied Arts** – *89 Southwark St. -* ⊖ *Southwark - closed Sun.* Here you'll find decorative art objects made by British designers.

69 **Neal's Yard Dairy** – *6 Park St. -* ⊖ *London Bridge - closed Sun.* A cheese factory selling only produce of Great Britain, including Cheddar, Stilton, Cashel Blue and many more of the excellent varieties produced in the UK.

NIGHTLIFE

80 **Ministry of Sound** – *not on the map - 103 Gaunt St. -* ⊖ *Elephant and Castle - closed Sun-Thu.* London's most famous nightclub offers a stunning experience, though one that calls for patience given the crowds. Expect to hear house music, garage and techno.

96 **Southbank Centre★** – *Belvedere Rd -* ⊖ *Waterloo - www. southbankcentre.co.uk.* Southbank Centre is Europe's largest centre for the arts, attracting more than three million visitors annually with with excellent acoustics and quality programming that includes classical and contemporary music as well as dance.

Addresses described in neighbouring sections:

16 **53** **77** ▶ *3*

38 ▶ *4*

23 ▶ *10*

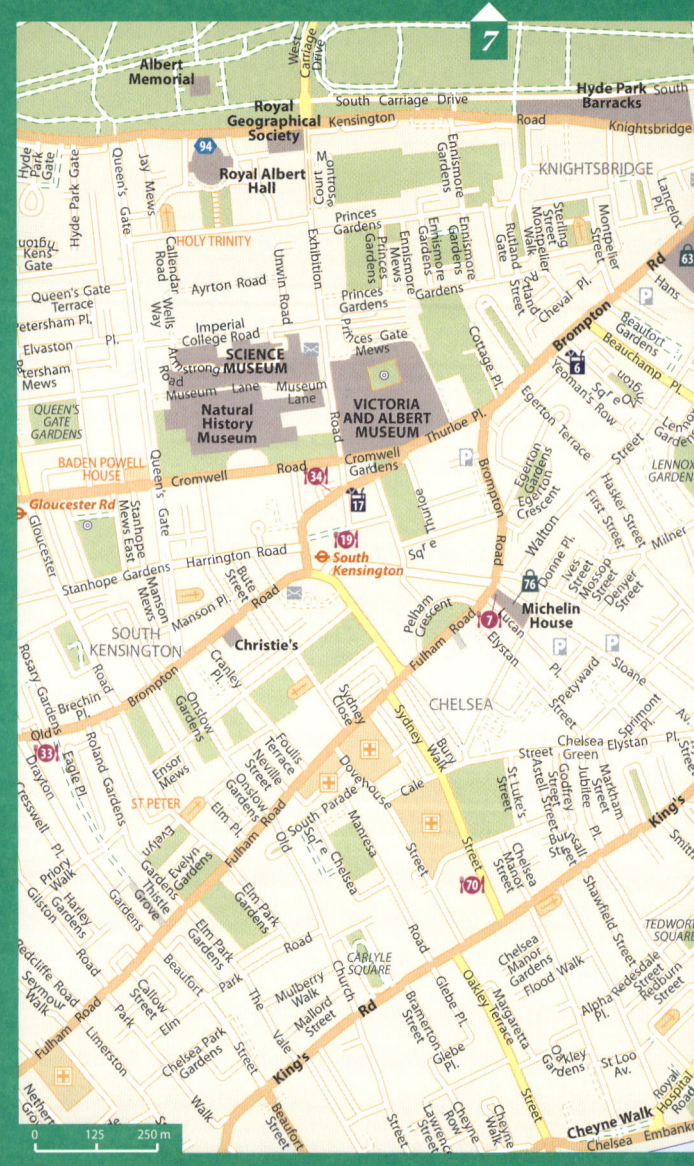

Albert Memorial

West Carriage Drive

South Carriage Drive

Hyde Park Barracks

South
Knightsbridge

Royal Geographical Society

Kensington

KNIGHTSBRIDGE

94

Royal Albert Hall

Montpelier Court

Ennismore Gardens

Ennismore Mews

Ennismore Gardens

Princes Gardens

Rutland Gate

Sterling Street

Montpelier Street

Montpelier Walk

Lancelot Pl.

63

Hyde Park Gate

Queen's Gate

Jay Mews

Hyde Park Gate

Rd

Hans

HOLY TRINITY

Lowther Kens. Gate

Queen's Gate Terrace

Exhibition

Rutland Gate

Cheval Pl.

Beaufort Gardens

Brompton

Beauchamp Pl.

6

Yeoman's Row

Lennox Gardens

Callendar Road

Wells Way

Ayrton Road

Unwin Road

Princes Gardens

Princes Gardens

Princes Gardens

Yeoman's Square

Sq're

Petersham Pl.

Imperial College Road

Elvaston Pl.

Petersham Mews

Armstrong Road

Museum Lane

Princes Gate Mews

Egerton Terrace

Hasker Street

First Street

Street

Milner

QUEEN'S GATE GARDENS

SCIENCE MUSEUM

Natural History Museum

Museum Lane

VICTORIA AND ALBERT MUSEUM

Cottage Pl.

Thurloe Pl.

Egerton Gardens

Egerton Crescent

Walton Street

LENNOX GARDENS

BADEN POWELL HOUSE

Queen's Gate

Cromwell

Road

34

Cromwell Gardens

Brompton Road

Ives Street

Donne Pl.

Mossop Street

Denyer Street

Gloucester Rd

Stanhope Mews East

17

Gloucester

Stanhope Gardens

Harrington Road

Manson Mews

Bute Street

19

Thurloe Sq're

Walton Pl.

76

Street

Road

South Kensington

Pelham Crescent

Milner Street

Hasker Street

SOUTH KENSINGTON

Manson Pl.

Road

Michelin House

Sloane Avenue

Brechin Pl.

Christie's

Cranley Pl.

Onslow Gardens

Sydney Close

Pelham Street

Fulham Road

7

Lucan Pl.

Elystan Pl.

Spetyward St.

CHELSEA

Sprimont Pl.

Ixworth Pl.

Rosary Gardens

Brompton

Foulis Terrace

Neville Street

Sydney Walk

Cale Street

Sydney Street

St. Luke's St.

Chelsea Green

Elystan St.

Markham Street

King's

Old Brompton

33

Roland Gardens

Ensor Mews

Onslow Gardens

Dovehouse Street

Astell Street

Jubilee Pl.

Godfrey Street

Burnsall Street

Smith

Cresswell Pl.

Drayton

Eagle Pl.

ST PETER

Elm Pl.

Old Church Street

South Parade

Manresa Road

Chelsea Manor Street

Shawfield Street

Evelyn Gardens

Thistle Grove

Elm Park Gardens

70

King's

Priory Walk

Harley Gardens

Gilston

Callow Street

Beaufort Street

Park

Elm Park Gardens

Road

Glebe Pl.

Chelsea Manor Gardens

Flood Walk

Margaretta Terrace

TEDWORTH SQUARE

Redesdale St.

Redcliffe Road

Seymour Walk

Fulham Road

Limerston Street

Chelsea Park Gardens

Beaufort Street

The Vale

Mulberry Walk

Mallord Street

CARLYLE SQUARE

Church Street

King's

Rd

Oakley Gardens

Alpha Pl.

St Loo Av.

Bramerton Street

Glebe Pl.

Lawrence Street

Cheyne Row

Cheyne Walk

Royal Hospital Road

Nether Gr.

Beaufort Street

Walk

King's

Cheyne Walk

Chelsea Embankment

WHERE TO EAT

Chelsea Farmers' Market 🔟
(125 Sydney St. - South Kensington, *Sloane Square)* – not a market at all – is a scenic square with one-off shops and restaurants with al fresco dining.

The **Market Place** *(9h-20h)* in particular has a pleasant shady terrace.

7 Bibendum Oyster Bar –
Michelin House - 81 Fulham Rd - South *Kensington -* 📞 *020 7581 5817 - www.bibendum.co.uk - menus £2831 (lunchtime), £36 (evening).* Located in Michelin House, this restaurant blends French and English cuisine; there's also an oyster bar.

19 Daquise – *20 Thurloe St. -* South Kensington *-* 📞 *020 7589 6117 - www.daquise.co.uk - dishes £15-20.* Quality Polish food at very reasonable prices and ideally located (100m from the museum).

33 Kare Kare – *152 Old Brompton Rd -* Gloucester Road *-* 📞 *020 7373 0024 - www.karekare.co.uk - dishes £9-15.* The lunch/evening menu (18h-19h30) at this Indian restaurant offers excellent value for money (£9.95).

24 Kulu Kulu Sushi – *39 Thurloe Pl. -* South Kensington *-* 📞 *020 7589 2225 - www.kulukulu.co.uk - allow £15-20.* Sushi and other Japanese small plates are prepared in an open kitchen and circulating along a conveyor belt.

TAKE A BREAK

6 Bunch of Grapes – **PUB** -
207 Brompton Rd - Knightsbridge. A short walk from Harrods, this beautiful Victorian-style pub is a place to relax between shopping sprees.

17 Greenfield's Café – *13-15 Exhibition Rd -* South Kensington -
closed evenings. In this adorable coffee shop, you can eat cakes, salads or sandwiches. Perfect for a break at lunch or tea time.

SHOPPING

Beauchamp Place, **Walton Street**, **Halkin Arcade**, **Brompton Road**, **Pont Street** and **Sloane Street** are lined with elegant shops.

63 Harrods – *87-135 Brompton Rd -* Knightsbridge. The famous department store prides itself on offering everything; it's almost like a museum. Don't miss the Food Hall, but note the dress code.

82 Harvey Nichols – *109-125 Knightsbridge -* Knightsbridge. Founded in 1831, this is one of the great London stores, offering high-end fashions, food and wine.

76 The Conran Shop – *Michelin House - 81 Fulham Rd -* South Kensington. The furniture store of designer Terence Conran (creator of Habitat) is installed here in the old Michelin offices.

NIGHTLIFE

94 Royal Albert Hall –
South Kensington, Knightsbridge *- www.royalalberthall.com.* Home of the Royal Philharmonic Orchestra, the Albert Hall also provides the setting for celebrated concerts (The Proms) in summer.

Suffused with a luxurious calm, these exclusive London districts are also renowned for the cultural and commercial pleasures they offer. Department stores and chic boutiques seduce those addicted to window shopping, while art lovers can explore the splendid Victoria and Albert Museum.

Royal Albert Hall

VISIT

Royal Albert Hall★ – ⊖ *South Kensington, Knightsbridge - www.royal alberthall.com.* Inaugurated in 1871, this circular domed red-brick structure is one of the most famous theatres in London (*Nightlife*).

Science Museum★★★ – *Exhibition Rd - ⊖ South Kensington - www.sciencemuseum.org.uk - 10h-18h.* This temple of science is remarkable for the wealth of its collections and the quality of its exhibitions.

Natural History Museum★★ – ⊖ *South Kensington - www.nhm.ac.uk - 10h-17h50.* Set in an imposing neo-Gothic building (1873-1880), this museum contains some 80 million objects and natural specimens in its vast collections.

Victoria and Albert Museum★★★ **(V&A)** – ⊖ *South Kensington - www. vam.ac.uk - 10h-17h45 (Fri 22h).* The V & A is dedicated to decorative arts across all eras and civilisations. There are nearly 2 million objects here ranged across 10km/6mi of galleries.

Christie's – *85 Old Brompton Rd - ⊖ South Kensington.* Founded in 1766, this auction house enjoys an international reputation.

Michelin House – *81 Fulham Rd - ⊖ South Kensington.* Occupied by Michelin until 1985, this 1910 building is notable for its windows bearing the image of Bibendum (also known as the Michelin Man). Today it houses the Conran Shop (*Shopping*) and a fine-dining restaurant.

Brompton Road – ⊖ *Knightsbridge.* At No. 135 on this bustling street is Harrod's★★ (*Shopping*), its interior resplendent with mosaics and stained glass.

Belgrave Square★★ – ⊖ *Hyde Park Corner.* Well-preserved, this square is built around a central garden and lined with historic houses and mansions.

Sloane Street – ⊖ *Knightsbridge, Sloane Square.* Built in 1773, this street is home to the Holy Trinity church (1888), decorated with beautiful stained glass windows designed by the Pre-Raphaelite Burne-Jones.

King's Road – ⊖ *Sloane Square.* Known for its boutiques, antique shops, restaurants and pubs, this street is also home to contemporary art at the Saatchi Gallery's (*www. saatchigallery.com - 10h-18h*).

Royal Hospital★★ – ⊖ *Sloane Square - www.chelsea-pensioners.org.uk - 10h-12h, 14h-16h - closed Sat-Sun.* Inspired by the Hotel des Invalides in Paris, this building has welcomed British war veterans since 1682.

Chelsea Physic Garden – *66 Royal Hospital Rd - ⊖ Sloane Square - www. chelseaphysicgarden.co.uk - Apr-Oct: daily except Mon and Sat 11h-18h - £9.90.* The oldest botanical garden in London, founded in 1673.

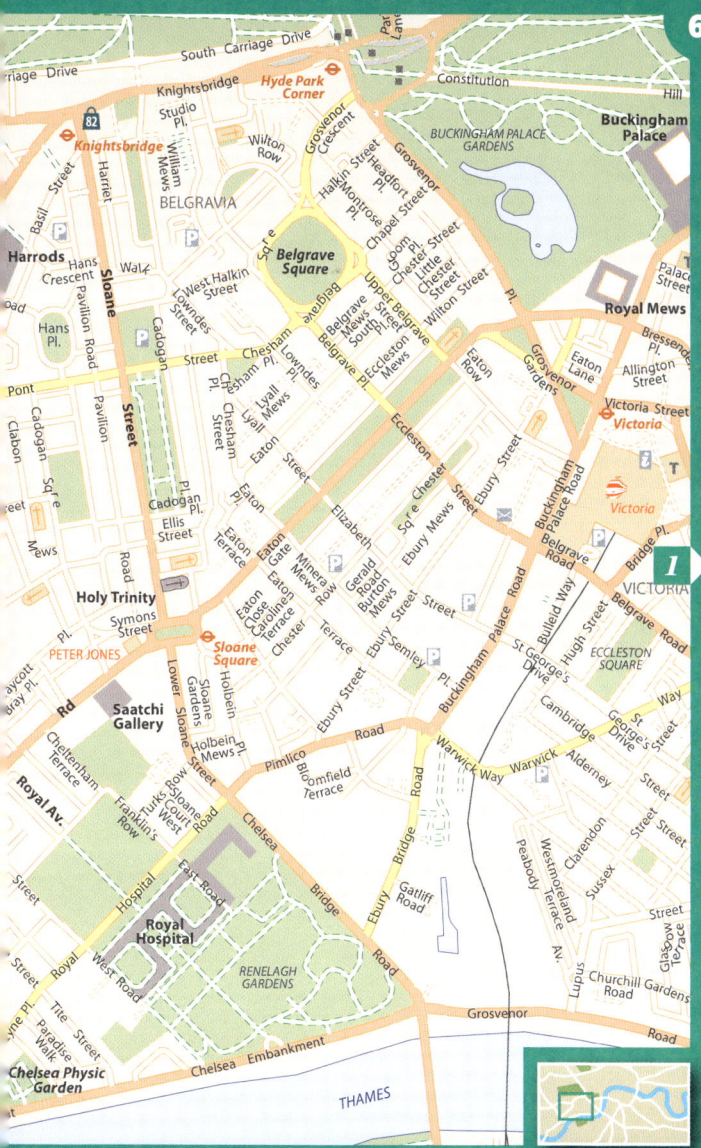

Hyde Park Corner

Constitution Hill

South Carriage Drive

Knightsbridge
Studio Pl.
William Mews

82 Knightsbridge

BUCKINGHAM PALACE GARDENS

Buckingham Palace

Basil Street

Harriet

Wilton Row

Grosvenor Crescent

Grosvenor

BELGRAVIA

Headfort Pl.
Halkin St.
Montrose Pl.
Chapel Street

Groom Pl.
Chester Street
Little Chester Street
Wilton Street

Pl.

Palace

Royal Mews

Harrods

Hans Crescent

Sloane

Pavilion Road

Walk

Cadogan

West Halkin Street

Lowndes Street

Belgrave Square

Upper Belgrave Street

Belgrave Mews South

Belgrave Pl.

Eccleston Mews

Eaton Row

Grosvenor Gardens

Eaton Lane

Bressenden Pl.

Allington Street

Hans Pl.

Pavilion

Chesham Street

Lowndes

Lyall Street

Lyall Mews

Eaton Street

Eccleston Street

Eaton Mews

Victoria Street

Victoria

Pont

Cadogan

Clabon

Sq.

Cadogan Pl.

Chesham Pl.

Chesham Street

Eaton Mews

Elizabeth Street

Sq.e Chester Street

Ebury Street

Buckingham Palace Road

Victoria

Ellis Street

Mews

Road

Cadogan Pl.

Eaton Terrace

Eaton Gate

Minera Mews

Gerald Road

Buxton Street

Ebury Street

Belgrave Road

Bridge Pl.

Holy Trinity

Symons Street

PETER JONES

Eaton Close

Eaton Terrace

Caroline Terrace

Chester

Ebury Street

Semley Pl.

St George's Drive

Bulleid Way

Hugh Street

VICTORIA

1

Sloane Square

ECCLESTON SQUARE

Saatchi Gallery

Rd

Cheltenham Terrace

Sloane Gardens

Lower Sloane Street

Holbein Pl.

Holbein Mews

Pimlico

Ebury Street

Road

Buckingham Palace Road

Warwick Way

Cambridge Street

Warwick Way

Warwick

George's Drive

Alderney Street

Way

Royal Av.

Franklin's Row

Turks Row

Sloane Court West

Blomfield Terrace

Bridge

Clarendon Street

Sussex Street

Hospital

East Road

Chelsea

Ebury

Gatliff Road

Westmoreland Terrace

Peabody Av.

Street

Glasgow Terrace

Street

Royal Hospital

West Road

Bridge Road

Churchill Gardens

Lupus Street

Road

Royal Av.

Tite Street

Paradise Walk

RENELAGH GARDENS

Grosvenor

Road

Chelsea Physic Garden

Chelsea Embankment

THAMES

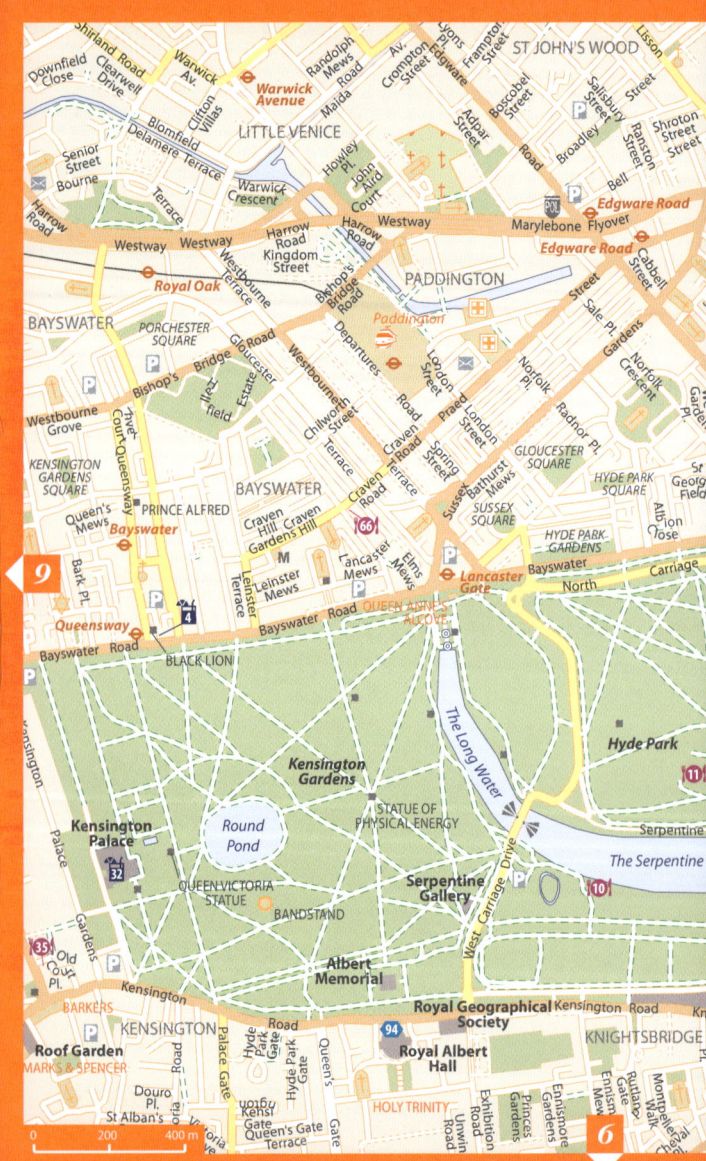

WHERE TO EAT

Several cafés and restaurants in **Hyde Park** serve snacks and hot meals: **The Serpentine Bar and Kitchen** 🍴, the **Lido café** 🍴 and the **Tennis Club café** 🍴 *(closed in the evening)*.

28 Golden Hind – *73 Marylebone Lane* - Bond Street - 020 7486 3644 - http://thegoldenhind.snack.ws - *closed Sun - dishes £11-15.* Some of the best fish and chips in London!

35 Maggie Jones – *6 Old Court Pl.-* High Street Kensington - 020 7937 6462 - www.maggie-jones.co.uk - *dishes £15-26.* This 19C country inn serves simple, honest home cooking; don't miss the pies and puddings.

36 Maroush I – *21 Edgware Rd* - Marble Arch - 020 7723 0773 - www.maroush.com - *dishes £15-20.* One of the oldest and best Lebanese restaurants in London.

66 Tukdin – *41 Craven Rd* - Lancaster Gate - 020 7723 6955 - www.tukdin.com - *dishes £10-20.* Excellent Malaysian cuisine mingling spicy flavours with Indian and Chinese influences.

TAKE A BREAK

Black Lion – **PUB** - *123 Bayswater Rd* - Queensway. This tavern has been welcoming visitors to Hyde Park for three centuries.

32 The Orangery – **TEA** - *Kensington Gardens* - High Street Kensington - *10h-18h (winter 17h).* This cafe is ideal for a coffee, a light lunch or an afternoon tea (from £24).

SHOPPING

Fans of window-shopping will delight in **Marylebone High St.**, **Oxford St.**, **Old & New Bond St.**, **South Molton St.** and **Savile Row**.

55 Daunt Books – *83 Marylebone High St.* - Baker Street. With its panelled gallery surmounted by a canopy, this Edwardian-style bookshop is one of the finest in the capital.

83 Selfridges – *400 Oxford St.* - Bond Street. You can find anything here, but the highlights are the fashion, beauty and food departments.

75 Stella McCartney – *30 Bruton St.-* Green Park - *closed Sun.* The talented designer's creations aren't within reach of every budget, but the shop is always worth a look.

80 Vivienne Westwood – *6 Davies St.* - Bond Street - *closed Sun* The temple for disciples of "Queen Viv", the designer who brought punk into the mainstream.

NIGHTLIFE

95 Wigmore Hall – *36 Wigmore St.* - Bond Street - www.wigmore-hall.org.uk. This intimate room has excellent acoustics. The Sunday morning coffee concerts are an institution.

Tea time

The green expanses of Hyde Park and Kensington Gardens together form the largest public park in London. To the east, Mayfair is the epitome of elegance and luxury, exemplified in the beautiful shop windows of Bond Street.

VISIT

Hyde Park★★ – ⊖ *Hyde Park Corner, Knightsbridge, Marble Arch.* Londoners flock to this huge park in droves at the first hint of sunshine. Orchestral recitals, boating on the Serpentine, horseriding and mini golf are among the warm-weather attractions.

Kensington Gardens★★ – ⊖ *Queensway, High Street Kensington.* To the west of Hyde Park, these beautifully landscaped gardens are highlighted by features like the Round Pond, the Orangery and the memorial fountain dedicated to Princess Diana.

Kensington Palace – ⊖ *Queensway, High Street Kensington - www.hrp.org.uk - 10h-18h - £16.50.* Queen Victoria lived here, as did the Prince Charles and Princess Diana. Formal wear, household objects and paintings form the core of the collections.

Albert Memorial★ – *Kensington Gardens.* Dedicated in 1876, this statue memorializes Queen Victoria's husband Albert, a promoter of the arts and education.

Serpentine Gallery – *Kensington Gardens - www.serpentinegallery.org - 10h-18h.* This pretty pavilion hosts exhibitions of contemporary art.

Oxford Street★ – ⊖ *Bond Street, Oxford Circus, Marble Arch.* Oxford Street extends east to Marble Arch and the corner of Hyde Park. This is a shopping street par excellence, home (at No. 400) to the famous **Selfridges** (⬙ *Shopping*).

The Squares★ – ⊖ *Baker Street.* **Montagu Square** (early 19C) is lined by homes whose ground floors are illuminated by small bow windows. **Bryanston Square**, which dates from the same era, is decorated with stucco terraces. To the east, **Gloucester Place** appeals with its alleys and wrought iron balconies.

Wallace Collection★★★ – *Hertford House, Manchester Square* - ⊖ *Bond Street - www.wallacecollection.org - 10h-17h.* At the heart of Marylebone, on a Georgian square, Hertford House features the French art collection of the 4th Marquess of Hertford (1800-1870).

New and Old Bond Streets★ – ⊖ *Bond Street.* Crossing Mayfair from north to south, Bond Street is the height of elegance, lined with luxury leather goods, fashion designers, chic stationery shops and art dealers.

Mount Street – ⊖ *Marble Arch, Hyde Park Corner.* Lined by tall, gabled brick houses adorned with terracotta details, this street offers antique furniture, paintings, porcelain and other assorted luxury goods.

Berkeley Square – ⊖ *Green Park.* This square built in 1737 features several well-preserved 18C houses.

Shepherd Market – ⊖ *Green Park.* Consisting of a maze of alleyways and courtyards connected by archways, this market has a village atmosphere, with period pubs, small houses and antique shops.

S. Frances/hemis.fr

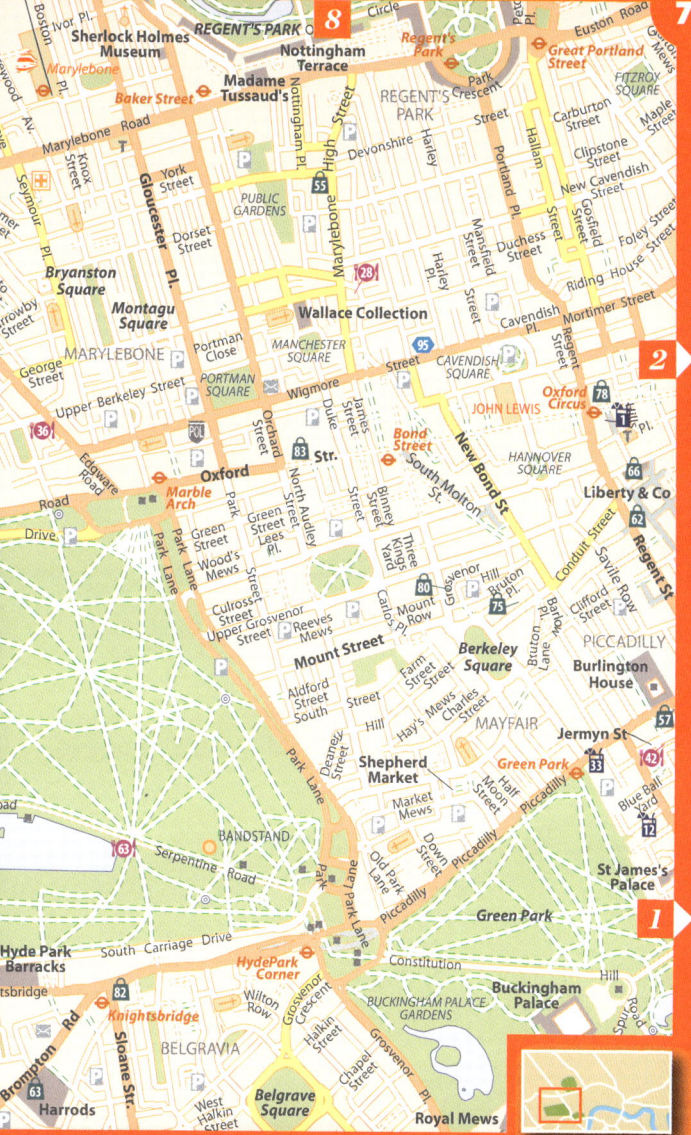

Boston Pl.
Ivor Pl.
Harewood Av.
Harewood Pl.
Marylebone

REGENT'S PARK

Sherlock Holmes Museum

8

Circle

Regent's Park

Euston Road

Great Portland Street

FITZROY SQUARE

Nottingham Terrace

Park Crescent

Madame Tussaud's

REGENT'S PARK

Baker Street

Carburton Street

Clipstone Street

New Cavendish Street

Gosfield St.

Foley Street

Marylebone Road

Grove
Seymour Pl.

York Street

Knox Street

Devonshire

Harley

Hallam

Portland Pl.

Riding House Street

PUBLIC GARDENS

55

Dorset Street

Mansfield St.

Duchess Street

Cato St.
Harrowby Pl.

Bryanston Square

Montagu Square

28

Harley Pl.

Cavendish Pl.

Mortimer Street

MARYLEBONE

Portman Close

Wallace Collection

95

CAVENDISH SQUARE

JOHN LEWIS

Oxford Circus

78

George Street

Upper Berkeley Street

PORTMAN SQUARE

MANCHESTER SQUARE

Street

1

Edgware Road

36

Wigmore

Duke

James

Bond Street

HANOVER SQUARE

66

Orchard Street

83

Oxford **Str.**

South Molton St.

New Bond St.

Liberty & Co

62

Marble Arch

North Audley Street

Binney Street

Regent St.

Drive
Road

Park Lane

Green Street

Lees Pl.

Three Kings Yard

Conduit Street

Savile Row

Wood's Mews

80

Grosvenor

Hill

Clifford Street

Culross Street

Upper Grosvenor Street

Reeves Mews

75

Bruton Pl.

Barlow Pl.

PICCADILLY

Mount Street

Carlos Pl.

Mount Row

Bruton Lane

Burlington House

Aldford Street South

Farm Street

Berkeley Square

Street

Street

57

Street

Hill

Hay's Mews

Charles Street

MAYFAIR

Jermyn St

Shepherd Market

Half Moon Street

Piccadilly

Green Park

33

42

Market Mews

12

Down Street

Blue Ball Yard

BANDSTAND

63

Old Park Lane

Piccadilly

St James's Palace

Serpentine Road

Park Lane

Deanery Street

Green Park

1

Hyde Park Barracks

South Carriage Drive

Constitution

Hill

Knightsbridge

HydePark Corner

82

Wilton Row

Grosvenor Crescent

BUCKINGHAM PALACE GARDENS

Buckingham Palace

Knightsbridge

BELGRAVIA

Halkin Street

Grosvenor Pl.

Brompton Rd.

Sloane Str.

West Halkin Street

Belgrave Square

Chapel Street

63

Harrods

Royal Mews

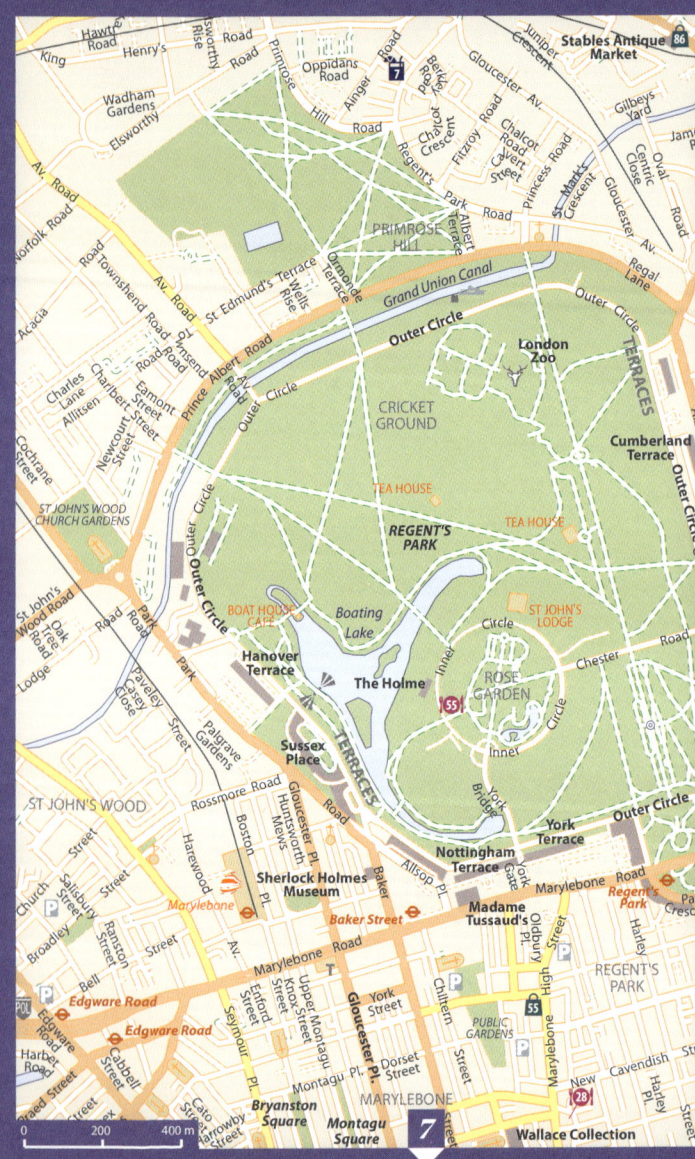

WHERE TO EAT

4 **Bar Gansa** – *2 Inverness St.
- ⊖ Camden Town - ℘ 020 7267 8909 -
www.bargansa.com - tapas £5-6, dishes
£12-17.* This tapas bar is one of the
most popular in Camden with a
flamenco show on Mondays.

24 **Dim T** – *32 Charlotte St. -
⊖ Goodge Street - ℘ 020 7637 1122 -
www.dimt.co.uk - dishes £8-12.* This
restaurant is known for cheap and
delicious dim sum and noodles.

40 **North Sea Fish Restaurant** –
*7-8 Leigh St. - ⊖ Russell Square - ℘ 020
7387 5892 - www.northseafishrestaurant.
co.uk - closed Sun - dishes £10-20.* Quality
fish and chips with home-made
tartare sauce.

47 **Tas** – *22 Bloomsbury St. - ⊖ Holborn
- ℘ 020 7637 4555 - www.tasrestaurants.
co.uk - dishes £8-14.* This Turkish
restaurant offers tasty dishes in
generous portions, with delicious
mezzes.

65 **The Café Garden** – *Queen Mary's
Gardens, Inner Circle - ⊖ Regent's Park,
Baker Street - ℘ 020 7935 5729 - www.the-
gardencafew1.com - closed in the evening -
dishes £10-15.* Enjoy sandwiches, salads
and other light fare in this cafeteria
surrounded by flowerbeds.

TAKE A BREAK

5 **Booking Office Bar** – **PUB** -
Euston Rd - ⊖ Kings Cross-St Pancras.
Set in the beautiful Gothic St Pancras
station, in the St Pancras Renaissance
Hotel, this bar-restaurant has
maintained the Victorian look of
what was once the station's booking
office. Stop in while you wait for
the Eurostar.

7 **Café Seventy Nine** – **TEA** -
79 Regent's Park Rd - ⊖ Chalk Farm. A
charming tea room that makes a nice
place to rest or enjoy a light lunch.

Camden Town Market

SHOPPING

52 **Camden Lock Market,
Camden Lock Village, Camden
Market** – *Chalk Farm Rd - ⊖ Camden
Town - 10h-18h.* You can find anything
in these lively weekend markets,
including clothes and accessories;
try Camden Lock Market for ethnic
crafts, jewellery and second-hand
goods.

86 **Stables Antique Market** –
*Chalk Farm Rd - ⊖ Camden Town -
weekend 10h-18h30.* A Housed in
former stables, this is a great place
for antique hunters (Art Deco,
1940-1950).

NIGHTLIFE

78 **Jazz Café** – *5 Parkway -
⊖ Camden Town - www.mamacolive.com/
thejazzcafe.* Jazz, soul and Latin
rhythms enliven evenings in this
club where many jazz greats have
played.

91 **The Forum** – *not on the map -
9-17 Highgate Rd - ⊖ Kentish Town.* An
Art Deco building transformed into
a concert hall that has seen Oasis,
Macy Gray and Iggy Pop.

Addresses described in section 7:
28 **55**

From the legendary Camden markets to the exceptional British Museum to the leafy Regent's Park, these neighbourhoods are full of contrasts; so much so that they're ideal both for families and those nostalgic for the glory days of punk rock.

Canal in Regent's Park

VISIT

British Museum★★★ – *Great Russell St. -* ⊖ *Tottenham Court Rd, Holborn - www.britishmuseum.org - 10h-17h30 (Fri 20h30).* Highlights here include the Far Eastern antiquities collections, the Ethnography Gallery (with a statue from Easter Island) and the archaeological collections (including the Rosetta Stone and sculptures from the Parthenon).

Bedford Square★★ – ⊖ *Tottenham Court Rd.* The most beautiful and best preserved of Bloomsbury squares.

Charles Dickens Museum – *Not on the map; to the east of the British Museum - 48 Doughty St. -* ⊖ *Russell Square - www.dickensmuseum.com - 10h-17h - £8.* Personal belongings and manuscripts are displayed in this 18C house where the British novelist lived, and wrote *"Oliver Twist"*.

British Library★★ – *96 Euston Rd -* ⊖ *King's Cross-St Pancras - www.bl.uk - 9h30-18h (Tue 20h, Sat 17h), Sun 11h-17h.* The National Library houses its treasures in the John Ritblat gallery, where you'll find three millennia of writings from around the world.

Regent's Park★★★ – ⊖ *Regent's Park.* Designed by John Nash, this early 19C park includes Queen Mary's Gardens as well as the restored William Andrews Nesfield's Avenue Gardens.

Terraces of Outer Circle★★ – ⊖ *Regent's Park.* At the edge of Regent's Park, and bordered by splendid palaces, the Outer Circle "terraces", are named after the titles of the children of George III. In a clockwise direction, the most remarkable are **Cumberland Terrace** (1826), **Chester Terrace** (1825) with its long façade punctuated by columns, **York Terrace** (1821), **Sussex Place** (1822), and **Hanover Terrace** (1823).

London Zoo★★ – *Regent's Park, Outer Circle -* ⊖ *Camden Town - www.zsl.org - 10h-17h30 (winter 16h) - £22.50.* Created in 1828, the zoo houses nearly 8,000 animals from 900 different species.

Madame Tussaud's – *Marylebone Rd -* ⊖ *Baker Street - www.madame-tussauds.com - during summer: 9h-19h (rest of year; call for details) - £30.* This famous wax museum presents effigies of celebrities from throughout history.

Sherlock Holmes Museum – *221B Baker St. -* ⊖ *Baker Street - www.sherlock-holmes.co.uk - 9h30-18h - £10.* This Victorian apartment was "inhabited" by the fictional Sherlock Holmes and Dr. Watson. A recommended visit for enthusiasts.

Camden Markets★ – *Chalk Farm Rd -* ⊖ *Camden Town - www.camdenlock.net - 10h-18h.* Camden attracts a motley crowd every weekend with its maze of markets (⚘ *Shopping*), vintage shops, food stands and the banks of its canal. It's one of the city's premiere attractions, though these markets are no longer what they were.

This West London village dating from the 19C is a popular middle-class neighbourhood, and has always attracted bargain hunters. Its bourgeois-bohemian (BoBo) atmosphere makes it one of the city's trendiest districts.

VISIT

Portobello Road★ – Notting Hill Gate, Ladbroke Grove. This winding street comes alive during the Saturday flea market, with the arrival of crowds in search of Victorian memorabilia, silverware, porcelain, stamps and other objects (Shopping).
In late August, Portobello Road is the rallying point of the Notting Hill Carnival.

Kensington Park Road – Notting Hill Gate, Ladbroke Grove. In recent years, Kensington Park Road has come to rival Portobello Road in terms of energy. Bars and restaurants have sprung up and remain open late into the night.

Museum of Brands, Packaging and Advertising★ – 2 Colville Mews – Paddington, Notting Hill Gate – www.museumofbrands.com – Tue-Sat 10h-18h, Sun 11h-17h – £6.50. This museum is dedicated to advertising through the ages.

Holland Park – Holland Park, High Street Kensington. The grounds of the beautiful **Holland House** (17C mansion, of which only the ground floor remains) are popular with London families who enjoy the ponds, shaded alleys, Japanese garden, children's playground and sports facilities.

Leighton House Museum★ – Not on the map; south of Holland Park – 12 Holland Park Rd – High Street Kensington – www.leightonhouse.co.uk –

Colourful houses in Notting Hill

10h-17h30 - closed Tue - £5. This house built in 1866 by the Orientalist Frederic Leighton (1830-1896), a painter and president of the Royal Academy, illustrates the Victorian aesthetic perfectly in its furnishings and amenities.

18 Stafford Terrace★ – not on the map - 18 Stafford Terrace - High Street Kensington - £8. Illustrator Linley Sambourne (1844-1910) moved into this house in 1875 and did much to embellish it. The rooms still have their original decor and furnishings.

WHERE TO EAT

202 – 202 Westbourne Grove - Notting Hill Gate - 020 7727 2722 - www.202london.com - closed Sun, and Mon evening - dishes £15-22. On the ground floor of this concept store by creator Nicole Fahri, you'll find a friendly café-restaurant with serving modern bistro essentials and diner classics as well as a wide range of internationally inspired dishes.

Beach Blanket Babylon – 45 Ledbury Rd - Notting Hill Gate - 020 7229 2907 - www.beachblanket.co.uk - dishes £15-35. Decor that's both medieval and Baroque creates a kitschy feel, but they take the modern Continental cuisine seriously, offering the likes of filet mignon and stew alongside pastas and risottos, with a full serving cocktails, wine and champagne.

25 E&O – *14 Blenheim Crescent -* ⊖ *Ladbroke Grove -* ℘ *020 7229 5454 - www.rickerrestaurants.com - dishes £10-30.* Deco design and music lounge that draws trendy clientele and serves Asian fusion cuisine.

68 Electric Diner – *191 Portobello Rd -* ⊖ *Ladbroke Grove -* ℘ *020 7908 9696 - www.electricdiner.com - dishes £9-20.* Next to the Electric Cinema, this buzzy spot sports American diner decor, with a long counter and red-leather booths, and a menu to match, with American-style comfort fare in generous portions.

27 Geales – *2 Farmer St. -* ⊖ *Notting Hill Gate -* ℘ *020 7727 7528 - www. geales.com - dishes £10-25.* There's a nautical theme at this longtimer (1939), a local institution that serves seafood and is especially popular with fans of fish and chips.

57 Modhubon – *29 Pembridge Rd -* ⊖ *Notting Hill Gate -* ℘ *020 7243 1778 - dishes £5-10.* A traditional tandoori restaurant, this place isn't much for decor, but with low prices and high quality Indian fare, it's a good choice for budget travellers.

41 Ottolenghi – *63 Ledbury Rd -* ⊖ *Notting Hill Gate -* ℘ *020 7727 1121 - www.ottolenghi.co.uk - 8h-20h (Sat 19h, Sun 18h) - dishes £20-25.* Fresh, delicious salads made with organic produce accompany diverse, creative entrees like smoked duck and eggplant and goat cheese quiche at this popular spot.

69 The Shed – *122 Palace Gardens Terrace -* ⊖ *Notting Hill Gate -* ℘ *020 7229 4024 - http://theshed-restaurant.com - closed Mon lunchtime and Sun - dishes £7-11.* The name is indicative of this restaurant's simple charms, which extend from rustic-chic decor tasty small plates that are perfect for sharing with friends.

TAKE A BREAK

29 The Grocer on Elgin – *6 Elgin Crescent -* ⊖ *Ladbroke Grove.* This grocery/takeaway offers very tempting prepared foods made with fresh seasonal produce. A small corner space allows you to eat in.

37 Tom's Delicatessen – *226 Westbourne Grove -* ⊖ *Notting Hill Gate - Thu-Sun 8h-18h30.* Opened by the son of designer Terence Conran, this slick coffee shop and grocery has a stylish aesthetic popular with the wealthy clientele of Notting Hill, who are attracted, at least in part, by the attractive display of cakes.

SHOPPING

50 Books for Cooks – *4 Blenheim Crescent -* ⊖ *Ladbroke Grove - closed Sun-Mon.* This bookshop is dedicated to the culinary arts. Just a step away, they opened a café with snacks and pastries, which is handy if shopping for cookbooks makes you hungry.

70 Oxfam – *245 Westbourne Grove -* ⊖ *Notting Hill Gate - 10h-18h, Sun 12h-14h.* Run by the charity organization, this shop sells almost-new cut-price clothing, often by various designers, as well as books and toys. The profits go to projects that help fight poverty around the world.

71 Paul Smith – *122 Kensington Park Rd -* ⊖ *Notting Hill Gate - closed Sun morning.* This eccentric outlet of the famous clothier is spread across four floors of a mansion, which is decorated with art and objects collected by Smith himself.

73 Portobello Road Flea Market – ⊖ *Notting Hill Gate, Ladbroke Grove - Sat 8h-17h.* From Notting Hill Gate to north of Portobello Road, antique shops are shoulder-to-shoulder with tat, Indian jewellery, crafts and a food market. Affordable souvenirs can be found alongside rare antiques and collectibles (old toys, jewellery, pottery, etc.) that go for exorbitant prices.

NIGHTLIFE

79 Lonsdale – *48 Lonsdale Rd - Notting Hill Gate - closed Sun-Mon.* Ranked on a list of the world's top 20 bars, this refined nightspot is tucked away from prying eyes in a quiet part of Notting Hill. Its chic patrons are drawn by stylish decor and elegant cocktails, and there are DJs Wednesday to Saturday.

81 Notting Hill Arts Club – *21 Notting Hill Gate - Notting Hill Gate - www.nottinghillartsclub.com - closed Sun-Mon.* This small club offers a variety of live music, sofas and a dance floor dark enough to make you shed your inhibitions and dance like nobody's watching.

90 The Electric Cinema – *191 Portobello Rd - Ladbroke Grove - www.electriccinema.co.uk.* This slightly retro cinema offers a varied programme of repertory and new releases. The immaculate interior, with two-seater sofas, leather armchairs and even double beds plus extensive food and drink offerings make for a unique cinema experience that's well worth the time.

Flea markets in Portobello Road

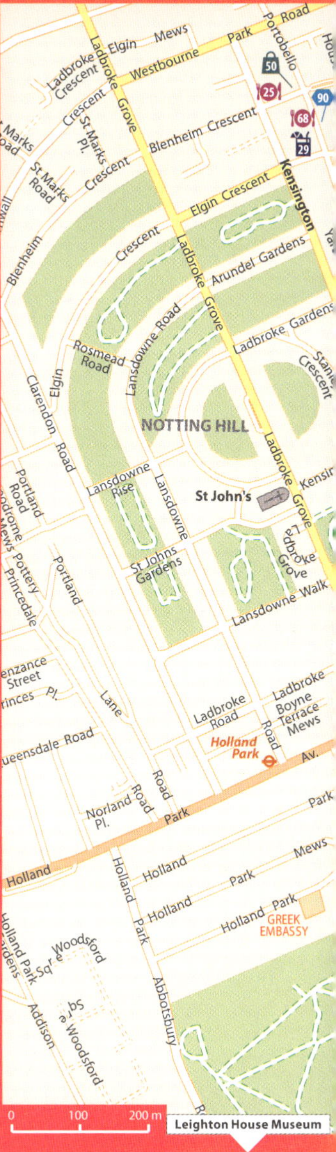

C. S. Pereyra/age fotostock

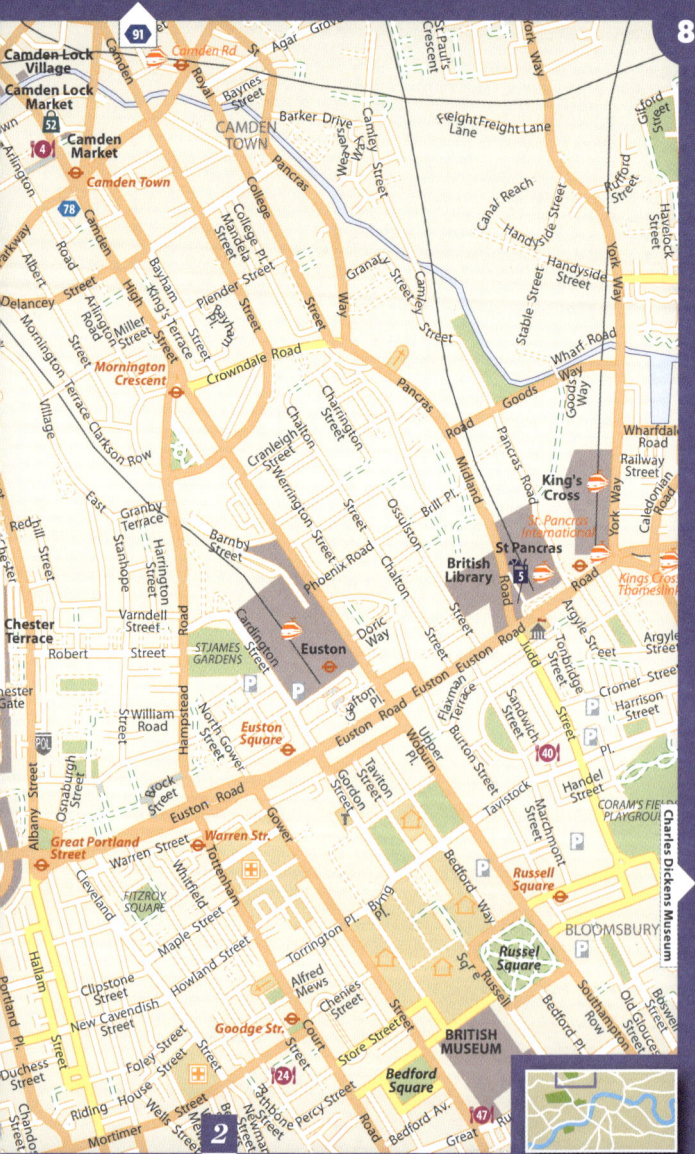

Camden Lock
Village
Camden Lock
Market
52
4 Camden
Market
Camden Town
78

Camden Rd
Royal
Baynes
Street
Barker Drive
CAMDEN
TOWN
Pancras
Agar Grove
St Pauls
Crescent
York Way
Freight
Freight Lane
Lane
Canal Reach
Rufford
Street
Gifford
Street
Havelock
Street

College Pl
Mandela
Street
Bayham Street
Plender Street
Bayham
Pl.
Granary
Street
Canley
Street
Handyside
Street
Stable Street
Handyside
Street
York Way

Mornington
Crescent
Crowndale Road
Pancras
Road
Midland
Road
Wharf Road
Goods
Way
Goods
Way
Goods
Way

Cranleigh St
Werrington Street
Charrington
Street
Chalton
Street
Ossulston
Street
Brill Pl.
Chalton
Pancras Road
King's
Cross
St Pancras
International
Wharfdale
Road
Railway
Street
Caledonian

Barnby
Street
Phoenix Road
Doric
Way
St Pancras
British
Library
5
Kings Cross
Thameslink
Argyle
Street

Chester
Terrace
ST JAMES
GARDENS
Cardington
Street
Euston
Grafton
Pl.
Argyle
Street
Cromer
Street
Tonbridge
Street
Sandwich
Street

Robert
Street
William
Road
North Gower Street
Euston Road
Euston
Square
Euston Road
Flaxman
Terrace
Burton Street
Harrison
Street
Handel
Street

Great Portland
Street
Warren Str.
Gower Street
Pavilion
Street
Gordon
Street
Upper Woburn Pl.
Tavistock
Marchmont Street
Russell
Square
CORAM'S FIELD
PLAYGROUND

40

Clipstone
Street
New Cavendish
Street
Maple Street
Howland Street
Tottenham Street
Alfred
Mews
Cleveland
FITZROY
SQUARE
Whitfield Street
Torrington Pl.
Byng Pl.
Bedford Way
Russel
Square
BLOOMSBURY
Charles Dickens Museum

Hallam
Duchess
Street
Foley Street
Riding
House
Street
Goodge Str.
Chenies
Mews
Store Street
Street
Rathbone
Court
Percy Street
24
Gower Street
Bedford
Square
BRITISH
MUSEUM
Bedford Sq
Russell Sq
Southampton Row
Old Gloucester
Bedford Row
Boswell
Street

Mortimer
Chandos
Great
Bedford Av.
47

Continuing growth on London's east side has contributed in the last few decades to significant redevelopment of the city's docks, with industrial spaces converted for residential use and plenty of new construction. Walks on the banks of the Thames and the Royal Greenwich Park make the Docklands a beautiful place to escape the whirlwind of the city.

St Katharine's Docks

VISIT

St Katharine's Docks★ – *DLR Tower Gateway.* This agreeable marina lined with offices, shops, restaurants and luxury apartments is particularly pleasant in summer.

Tobacco Dock★ – *DLR Shadewell.* A former bonded warehouse (1811-1813), this building is worth a look for its beautiful vaulted brick and metal structure. It's now one of London's most versatile events venues.

Museum of London Docklands★ – *West India Quay - DLR West India Quay, Canary Warf - www.museumoflondon.org.uk - 10h-18h.* This museum traces the history of the Docklands across the centuries, offering a better understanding of what they are today.

Canary Wharf★★ – *DLR Canary Wharf.* The rebirth of Canary Wharf, now a premier business district, began in 1988 with the construction of the first skyscrapers, including **One Canada Square** (235m), commonly known as **Canary Wharf Tower**.

Isle of Dogs★ – *DLR West India Quay, Canary Wharf.* This spit of land in a bend of the Thames came by its name when King Henry VIII established kennels here in the 16C. The creation of the West India Import Docks transformed the area in the early 19C. The docks closed in the 1980s, but the island was renewed again, thanks in part to the growth of Canary Wharf.

Cutty Sark★★ – *King William Walk - DLR Cutty Sark - www.rmg.co.uk - 10h-17h - £12.* Built on the Clyde, Scotland, in 1869, this majestic three-masted ship was created to import tea from China.

National Maritime Museum★★★ – *Romney Rd - DLR Cutty Sark - www.rmg.co.uk - 10h-17h - no charge; planetarium and Royal Observatory £11.50.* This museum's fabulous collections (inclduing coins, rare instruments and other treasures) illustrate the naval history of Great Britain.

Old Royal Naval College★★ – *King William Walk - DLR Cutty Sark - 8h-18h; Painted hall and chapel: 10h-17h.* The former Royal Naval College is notable for its Painted Hall, the old refectory capped with a dome (completed in 1703), and its chapel.

Queen's House★★ – *DLR Cutty Sark - www.nmm.ac.uk - 10h-17h.* This elegant white-walled villa hosts temporary exhibitions.

Royal Observatory Greenwich ★★ – *Blackheath Ave. - DLR Cutty Sark - www.nmm.ac.uk - 10h-17h.* Located in Greenwich Park, the Observatory invites visitors to see the Flamsteed House, home of the Astronomer Royal John Flamsteed, the Meridian Building which houses a collection of instruments, and to see the earth by means of the digital laser projector in the Peter Harrison Planetarium.

The O2 – ⊖ North Greenwich - www.theo2.co.uk. Named after the telecom company O2, but also known as the Millennium Dome, this concert arena was designed by Richard Rogers and is topped by an impressive fibreglass roof.

WHERE TO EAT

21 Davy's Wine Vaults – 161 Greenwich High Rd - DLR Greenwich - ☎ 020 8858 9147 - www.davyco.uk - dishes £10-30. The Greenwich outlet of a London wine merchant, this restaurant offers British fare and a wide selection of wines in a rustic, family friendly setting.

23 Dickens Inn – Marble Quay, St Katharine's Way - ⊖ Tower Hill - ☎ 020 7488 2208 - www.dickensinn. co.uk - dishes £11-25. Opened in 1976 by the grandson of Charles Dickens, this typical pub with 18C-style decor serves pasta and gigantic pizzas .

30 Inside – 19 Greenwich South St. - DLR Greenwich - ☎ 020 8265 5060 - www.insiderestaurant.co.uk - closed Mon - dishes £15-23. A refined but understated setting coupled with inventive, well-executed European cuisine make this one of the best restaurants in Greenwich.

43 Rivington – 178 Greenwich High Rd- DLR Greenwich - ☎ 020 8293 9270 - www. rivingtongreenwich.co.uk - closed Mon-Wed lunchtimes - dishes £13-30. Located in the Picturehouse complex, the Rivington offers typically English cuisine, including a hearty English breakfast.

60 The Gun – 27 Coldharbour - DLR Canary Wharf - ☎ 020 7515 5222 - www.thegundocklands.com - dishes £15-55. This pub has a long association with smugglers who would land contraband on the site and distribute it via a hidden tunnel. Today it offers fine cuisine and a riverside terrace.

62 The Prospect of Whitby – 57 Wapping Wall - ⊖ Wapping - ☎ 020 7481 1095 - www.taylor-walker.co.uk - dishes £10-15. A former haunt of bandits, this place serves classic pub food (burgers, pies, fish and chips) and offers a terrace overlooking the river.

TAKE A BREAK

At **Canary Wharf**, pubs and small bars invite you to stop by for a drink, an ice cream or a slice of pie.

21 Royal Teas Café – 76 Royal Hill - DLR Greenwich. A discrete, cosy and intimate vegetarian café and coffee shop at the heart of Greenwich.

28 The Grapes – PUB - Limehouse - 76 Narrow St. - DLR Westferry. Once frequented by Dickens, this charming historic pub and dining room has two tiny terraces overlooking the river.

SHOPPING

61 Greenwich Market – DLR Cutty Sark. Established since 1700, this covered market has art booths, crafts, food (daily except Mon and Thu 10h-1730h), and second-hand goods (Tue, Thu and Fri 10h-1730h).

> **Addresses described in section 4:**
> **13 38**

Greenwich Park and the Royal Observatory

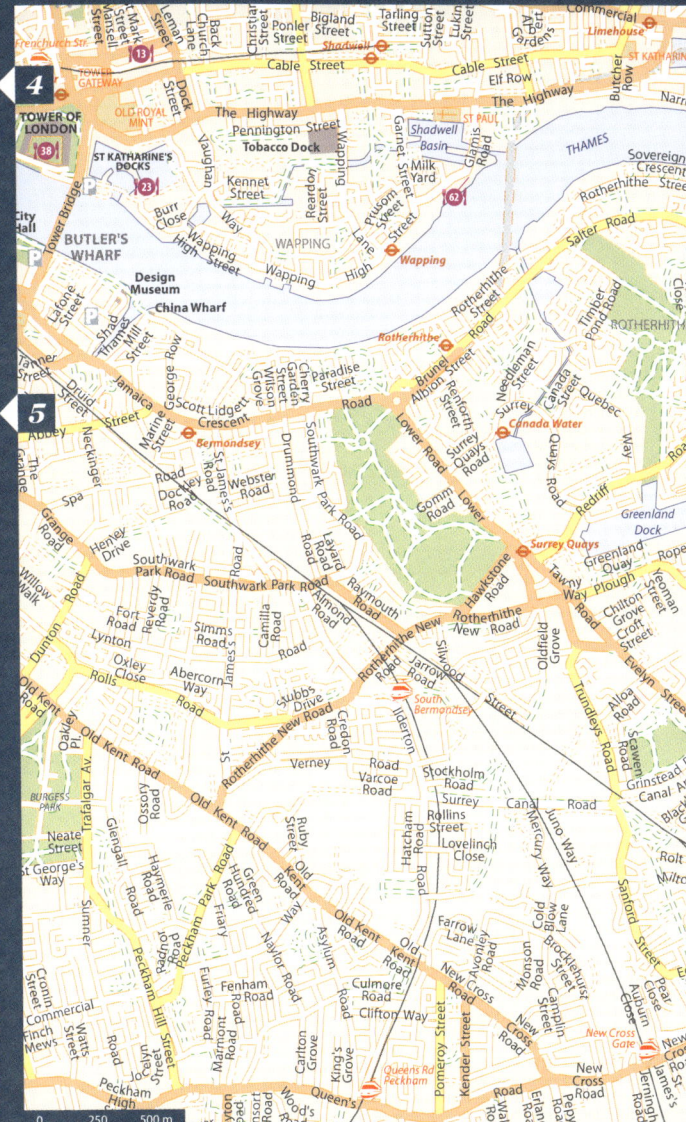

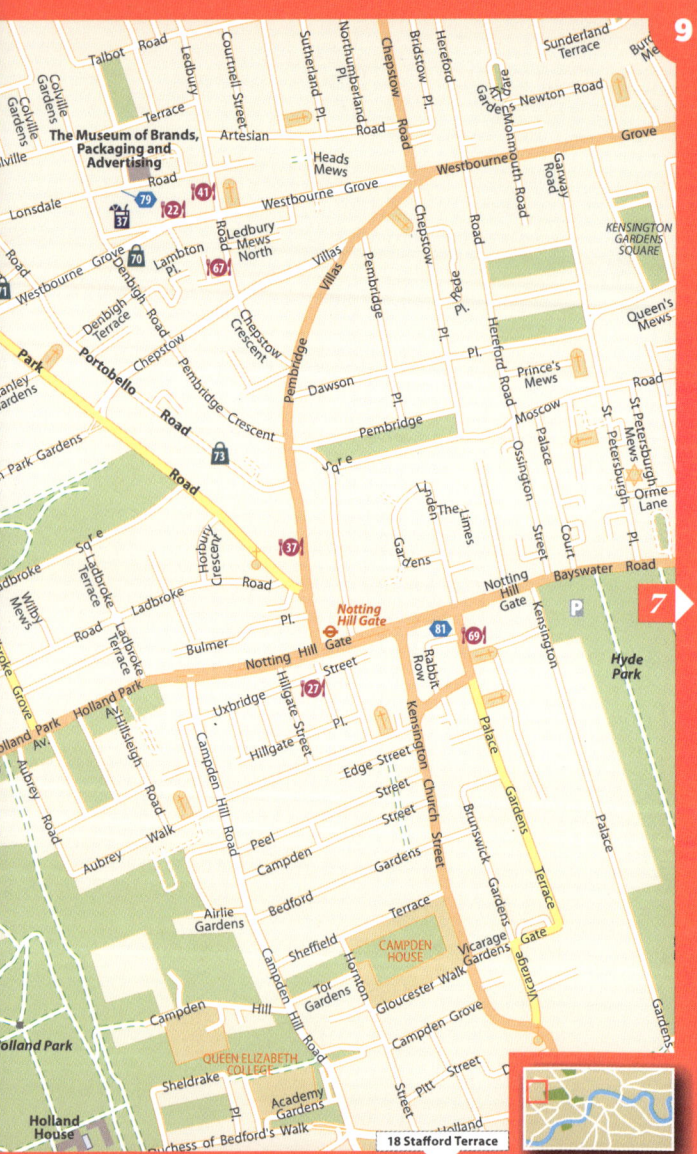

The Museum of Brands, Packaging and Advertising

KENSINGTON GARDENS SQUARE

Queen's Mews

St Petersburgh Place

Orme Lane

Prince's Mews

Moscow Place

Ossington Street

Court

Notting Hill Gate

Bayswater Road

Hyde Park

Notting Hill Gate

Kensington

Hyde Park

CAMPDEN HOUSE

QUEEN ELIZABETH COLLEGE

Holland Park

Holland House

Talbot Road
Colville Gardens
Colville Gardens
Colville
Lonsdale
Ledbury
Terrace
Courtnell Street
Sutherland Pl.
Northumberland Pl.
Chepstow Road
Bridstow Pl.
Hereford Road
Monmouth Road
Newton Road
Sunderland Terrace
Garway Road
Grove
Artesian
Heads Mews
Westbourne Grove
Westbourne Park Road
Westbourne Grove
Denbigh Terrace
Denbigh Road
Lambton Pl.
Ledbury Mews North
Chepstow Villas
Pembridge Villas
Chepstow Crescent
Pembridge Crescent
Pembridge Road
Chepstow Place
Hereford Pl.
Dawson Pl.
Pembridge Square
Stanley Gardens
Ladbroke Gardens
Portobello Road
Kensington Park Gardens
Ladbroke Square
Horbury Crescent
Ladbroke Road
Wilby Mews
Bulmer Pl.
Notting Hill Gate
Uxbridge Street
Hillgate Street
Hillgate Place
Hillgate Street
Hillsleigh Road
Holland Park Av.
Aubrey Road
Aubrey Walk
Campden Hill Road
Peel Street
Campden Street
Bedford Gardens
Airlie Gardens
Sheffield Terrace
Campden Hill
Tor Gardens
Hornton Street
Gloucester Walk
Campden Grove
Vicarage Gardens
Vicarage Gate
Edge Street
Kensington Church Street
Brunswick Gardens
Palace Gardens Terrace
Palace Gardens
The Limes Gardens
Lynden
Pembridge Square
Sheldrake
Campden Hill Road
Academy Gardens
Duchess of Bedford's Walk
Pitt Street
Holland

WHEN TO GO

Seasons

Throughout the year, temperatures in London are moderate, often with high humidity. The best times to visit are **spring** and **late autumn** when temperatures are mild. **Festivals** attract crowds in summer and the winter holiday season is popular too, with prices inflated from **Christmas through the turn of the year** and **into January.** Avoid this period if you don't like crowds.

Calendar

London Parade – *1 Jan.* New Year Parade, starting at 12h from Parliament Square to Piccadilly.

Chinese New Year – *Feb.* In Chinatown, in Soho.

Gay Pride London – *Jul.* From Oxford Street to Trafalgar Square.

Notting Hill Carnival – *Last weekend of August.* Great Caribbean carnival, starting in Portobello Road.

London Open House – *Sep.* National Heritage Days.

Guy Fawkes Night – *5 Nov.* Firework displays in all the main parks.

🕮 For more information, visit the Office of Tourism: www.visitlondon.com.

HOW TO GET THERE

By air

London is served by five airports, all at some distance from the capital.

Heathrow – www.heathrowairport. com. To reach London: **Underground** Piccadilly Line (50 minutes to Piccadilly Circus, £5); **National Express bus** (journey 35-50mn, £6); or **Heathrow Express** (15-20mn to Paddington, £20). By **taxi**, allow £70.

Gatwick – www.gatwickairport.com. To reach London: **National Express**

St Pancras station

bus (1h30, £8) or **Gatwick Express** (30-35mn to Victoria, £19.90). By **taxi**, allow £95.

Luton Airport – www.london-luton. co.uk. To get to London: Luton **shuttle** to Luton station (£1.50) then **train** to St Pancras and King's Cross (£13), by **taxi**, allow £90.

Stansted Airport – www.stansted airport.com. To reach London: **Stansted Express bus** to Liverpool Street Station (45-50mn, £23.40). By **taxi**, allow £90.

London City Airport - www.london cityairport.com. To reach London: **DLR** (Docklands Light Railway) to Bank (22mn) – connection with the **underground**). By **taxi**, allow £35.

By rail

St Pancras station – Arrival point for **Eurostar**: www.eurostar.com.

By bus

Eurolines – www.eurolines.co.uk.

> ### Check list
>
> **Formalities:** Identity card or valid passport.
>
> **Currency:** Pound sterling (£). In September 2015, £1 = €1.37 and $1.53.
>
> **Time:** British Summer Time applies: March-October.
>
> **Electricity:** 240V: three-pin plug (adapter required).

GETTING AROUND LONDON

Transport for London – ☎ 0843 222 1234 (24h/24) - www.tfl.gov.uk.

The Underground

The Underground, also commonly known as the Tube, is by far the fastest way to get around the capital.

Network - Twelve lines identified by a name and a colour that even serve Heathrow Airport and some towns and suburbs in Greater London. Cardinal directions (Northbound, Southbound, Eastbound and Westbound) help clarify the line's destination.

The **Docklands Light Railway** (DLR) is an independent line without drivers, serving East London from the City.

Operating hours: Monday-Saturday 5h/5h30 to 0h30/1h, Sunday 7h to 0h/0h30.

London Overground

London Overground rail service is a suburban rail network that serves a large part of Greater London, and enables visitors to explore attractions away from the city centre, or to find less costly accommodation outside of the centre and then travel in.

Bus

Red double-decker bus: These transport icons are a charming fixture on London's streets and allow you to better explore the capital. The network has about 130 lines. To make the most of it, get the free Central London map, available at Underground stations.

Night bus: Identified by the letter N preceding the route number, these buses take over from the Underground and day buses between 0h00 and 7h. The schedules are irregular, but you can signal the driver to stop.

Tickets

Public transport is quite expensive. Moreover, prices vary depending on the area and the time of travel.

Ticket Types - The full fare ticket (peak ticket) allows all-day travel. An off-peak ticket can be used at weekends and holidays, but only between 9h30 and 16h30 from Monday to Friday.

To buy - In tube stations or vending machines next to bus stops. If you travel without a valid ticket, the fine can be up to £80.

Prices - An Underground ticket costs £4.50, a bus ticket £2.40. So it is better to opt for a card (☘ *Tips*).

In case of emergency

European emergency number: ☎ 112

Emergencies: ☎ 999

Lost or stolen credit cards: Amex: ☎ 0 800 587 6023; Visa: ☎ 0 800 891 725; Master Card: ☎ 0 800 964 767.

Lost property: ☎ 0 845 330 9882 (Transport for London)

Health: to contact a doctor, get the number of a 24/24 hospital or medical information: NHS - ☎ 0845 46 47 (free call) - www.nhs.uk; Medicentre - ☎ 0 845 437 0353 - www.medicentre.co.uk.

By bike

Barclays Cycle Hire – A self-service bicycle system is now available in London. Payment is by credit card, with the first 30 minutes free.
Be very careful when you ride in the city centre, as traffic is particularly intense. A cycle network is being developed in some areas of the capital. London Cycle Guide guides, available in Travel Information Centres, suggest cycle routes.

By taxi

Many London taxis, historically black, now sport flashy colours. You can hail them in the street when the amber "For hire" roof sign is lit. Taxis use meters, with the fare based on distance travelled and some standard charges. Rates increase after 20h, and on weekends and holidays.
You can make reservations by calling this number: 🖉 0871 871 8710 (approx £2).

MONEY

Banks and exchange - banks and ATMs are plentiful in the city centre. Banks are generally open Monday to Friday from 9h30 to 16h30. Credit cards are accepted at most establishments (with the exception of some B&Bs; be sure to check).

Budget - London is a very expensive destination. Count on an average of £100 for one night in a bed and breakfast, £12 for fish and chips in a pub, from £20 for a ticket to musical, £4 for a beer and £15 for a temporary exhibition in a large museum.

Tipping - A service charge (12.5%) is usually included in the bill at restaurants and bars. If it's not, it is customary to leave a tip of 10-15%. Taxi drivers appreciate something (about 10-15%), and you won't begrudge giving them a tip when they have been particularly helpful and informative — you can learn a lot from the taxi drivers.

TIPS

Museums and monuments - In London, unless otherwise stated, all museums are free. Some of them offer combined tickets that allow you to visit several sites at an attractive rate.

London Pass - www.londonpass.com. On sale in information centres or on the Internet, the Pass entitles free entry and fast access to nearly 55 sites, museums and attractions. Prices: 1 day (£52), two days (£71) or 3 days (£85). With unlimited travel on the entire London transit network: £65, £89, £113.

Public transport - The Travelcard provides unlimited access to the metro, buses and commuter trains. One Day Travelcard (1 day): £12 in zones 1 and 2 (peak ticket). Seven Day Travelcard (7 days): £32.10 in zones 1 and 2 (peak ticket).

The **Visitor Oyster card** is a prepaid card that can be used throughout London's transit network. It stores an amount of money and is rechargeable as necessary at branches of Underground stations, on the Internet (www.tfl.gov.uk/oyster) and at many retailers. With this card, the subway and bus rides for zones 1-2 amounts to £2.90 (peak); as a guide, purchase a £10 credit for one day, £15 for two days and £20 for three days. You will need a card for each person.

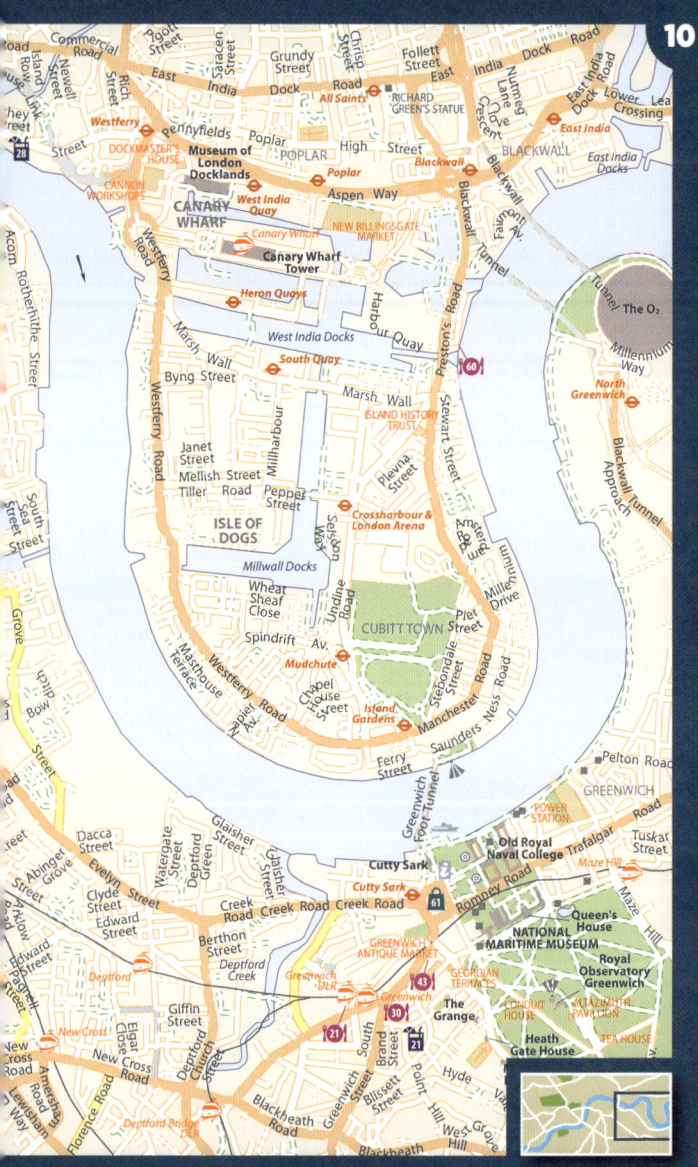

INDEX

No. of section ——→

Covent Garden . . . . **2 L**

L: left page map
C: centre spread map
R: right page map

MICHELIN

Michelin Travel Partner

Société par actions simplifiées au capital de 11 288 880 EUR
27 cours de l'Ile Seguin - 92100 Boulogne Billancourt (France)
R.C.S. Nanterre 433 677 721

No part of this publication may be reproduced in any form
without the prior permission of the publisher.

© Michelin Travel Partner
Printer: Book Partners China
Printed in China: 11-2015 ISO 14001

Food - There are many economic ways to eat in London: fresh salad bars and shelves of supermarkets (try Marks & Spencer, Sainsbury's and Tesco); fresh produce markets – Borough Market Camden Market, Portobello Road Market, etc.; snacks and coffee chains like Starbucks, Caffè Nero, Eat and Ready to Eat. You can eat here for as little as £5-10.

Many restaurants offer a lunch menu consisting of two or three dishes at good value.

Theatre - www.tkts.co.uk. The booth in Leicester Square is the only one to offer half-price tickets.

OPENING HOURS & PUBLIC HOLIDAYS

Stores and shops - Monday-Saturday 9h30/10h-18h/19h, sometimes later for department stores. Most open on Sunday (10h/11h-16h/17h) in tourist areas. Others open at night (20h/21h) on Wednesdays (Knightsbridge, Chelsea) or Thursdays (Oxford Street, Kensington High Street, Covent Garden).

Pharmacies - 9h-18h. Late-opening pharmacy: Bliss Pharmacy - 5-6 Marble Arch - ⊖ Marble Arch - ☎ 020 7723 6116.

Museums and monuments - 10h-18h. Many open every day of the week, although their hours are sometimes reduced on Sundays and public holidays (Bank Holidays), but most close on 1 Jan and 25-26 December

Holidays - 1 January (New Year's Day); Good Friday; Easter Monday; first Monday of May (May Bank Holiday); last Monday in May (Spring Bank Holiday); last Monday in August (August Bank Holiday); 25 December (Christmas Day); 26 December (Boxing Day).

WHERE TO EAT

Facilities - There are pubs, gastro pubs and restaurants.

Most establishments serve from 12h to 14h/14h30 and from 18h30 to 22h/22h30. Pubs close at 23h/midnight on weekdays and 22h30 on Sundays.

Specialities - The traditional English breakfast is usually served in hotels and B&Bs.

Do not miss fish and chips, the Cornish pasty (pie with meat and potatoes) and other hearty savory pies. The trifle (sponge cake, custard, whipped cream and fruit) is something to discover, although you might want to think twice about jellied eels, a popular London delicacy.

SHOWS

Programming - Check out the Evening Standard newspaper or the Time Out website: www.timeout.com/london.

Booking - Tickets for shows, concerts and sporting events are available on www.ticketmaster.co.uk or www.keithprowse.com.

The English way

From 16h onwards, it's tea time: pastries and mini sandwiches served with a cup of tea.

It is customary to have a beer in a pub after work, at 17h-18h, or before going out to dinner (19h30-21h).

This website is dedicated to theatre: www.officiallondontheatre.co.uk.

Tickets are available at reduced rates at the TKTS booth in Leicester Square.

Venues - To see a musical, you must go to the West End, around Soho and Covent Garden. Lovers of classical music will enjoy themselves at the Albert Hall (🏛 *Section 6*), or even at the Royal Opera House (🏛 *Section 2*).

TOURS & THINGS TO DO

Cruises - City Cruises (📞 020 7740 0400 - www.citycruises.com); Bateaux London (📞 020 7695 1800 - www.bateauxlondon.com). For more information, visit Transport for London (www.tfl.gov.uk).

Amphibious vehicle - Themed routes including part on the River Thames: London Duck Tours - 📞 020 7928 3132 - www.londonducktours.co.uk.

Walking - There are numerous guides available for walking tours in London, which, for such a large city, offers more opportunity for walking than you might imagine. Check in any of the major book stores.

TELEPHONE AND INTERNET

Call to Great Britain - 00 📞 + 44 + number you're calling, without the first 0 (i.e. 10 digits).

Weights and measures

1 pound = 0,5 kg

1 mile = 1.61 km

Size 10 (clothes) = 6 US

Shoe size 5 = 7 US

Calling abroad from London - 📞 00 = country code (1 for USA/ Canada) + number you're calling.

WiFi - In addition to the hotels, cafés and restaurants, some museums or parks offer wireless internet access. Free WiFi is increasingly provided at numerous outlets.

Editorial Director: Cynthia Ochterbeck
Editorial: Camille Bouvet, Anna Crine
Contributing Writers: Terry Marsh, Dave Zuckerman, Anna Crine, Matilde Miñon-Marqua, María Guttiérez-Alonso, Guylaine Idoux, Hervé Kerros, Sarah Larrue, Sarah Parot, Pierre Plantier
Cartography: Laurence Sénéchal, Daniel Duguay
Cover & Interior Design: Laurent Muller
Additional Layout: Natasha George
Photo research: Yoshimi Kanazawa, Marie Simonet, Maria Gaspar

Special Sales: travel.lifestyle@us.michelin.com
Contact us: Michelin Travel & Lifestyle North America, One Parkway South, Greenville, SC 29615, USA
travel.lifestyle@us.michelin.com

Michelin Travel Partner, Hannay House, 39 Clarendon Road, Watford, Herts WD17 1JA, UK
travelpubsales@uk.michelin.com
www.ViaMichelin.com

Printed: October 2015

WHERE TO STAY

London is a huge, sprawling urban area, so it's important to select your base depending on your budget and the sights and areas you intend to visit. Continue reading for more information about specific accommodation types to find one that meet your needs and your budget.

University Residences - Excellent solution for budget accommodation, offering low prices during school holidays: International Students House (www.ish.org.uk), University of Westminster (www.westminster. ac.uk), University College London (www.ucl. ac.uk).

Hostels - Hostelling International (www.hihostels.com); Youth Hostel Association (www.yha.org.uk).

Hotels - www.londontown.com; www.lhts.com; www.bhrc.co.uk.

There is also a selection of hotels on www.viamichelin.co.uk or www.booking.com.

Bed & Breakfast - Family style accommodations offering only a few rooms at moderate prices. Bookings: London Home-to-Home (www.londonhometohome.com); London Bed & Breakfast Agency (www.londonbb.com); Up Town Reservation (www.uptownres.com).

Apartment rental - An ideal solution for longer stays. Reservations on www.homelidays.com; www.airbnb.com. ♿ See also www.visitlondon.com.

RHYMING COCKNEY SLANG

Cockney rhyming slang is a form of phrase construction especially prevalent in dialectal English from the East End of London; hence the name, Cockney rhyming slang. The construction involves replacing

Tourist Information

Online:
www.visitbritain.com (tourist from Great Britain)
www.visitlondon.com (tourist office in London)

On site:
City of London Information Centre – St Paul's Churchyard – ⊖ St Paul's – ℰ 020 7332 1456 – www.visitthecity.co.uk.
London Travel Information Centres – King's Cross-St Pancras and Piccadilly Circus.

a familiar word or phrase with a rhyming phrase of two or three words and then, in almost all cases, omitting the secondary rhyming word. It makes the meaning of the phrase bewildering to anyone not in the know, but is a fascinating part of the London ethos. Here are a few examples that you might hear while out and about:

apples and pears	**stairs**
kettle and hob	**watch**
Adam and Eve	**believe**
Ruby Murray	**curry**
Butcher's Hook	**look**
Trouble and Strife	**wife**
Barnet Fair	**hair**
Dog and Bone	**phone**
Jack Jones	**alone**
Ball and Chalk	**walk**
Barney Rubble	**trouble**
Bees and Honey	**money**
Boat Race	**face**
Dinky Doos	**shoes**
Dicky Dirt	**shirt**
Loaf of bread	**head**
Jam jar	**car**
Whistle and flute	**suit**
Rosy Lee	**tea**
Rub-a-Dub	**pub**
Hank Marvin	**starving**
Dog's Meat	**feet**

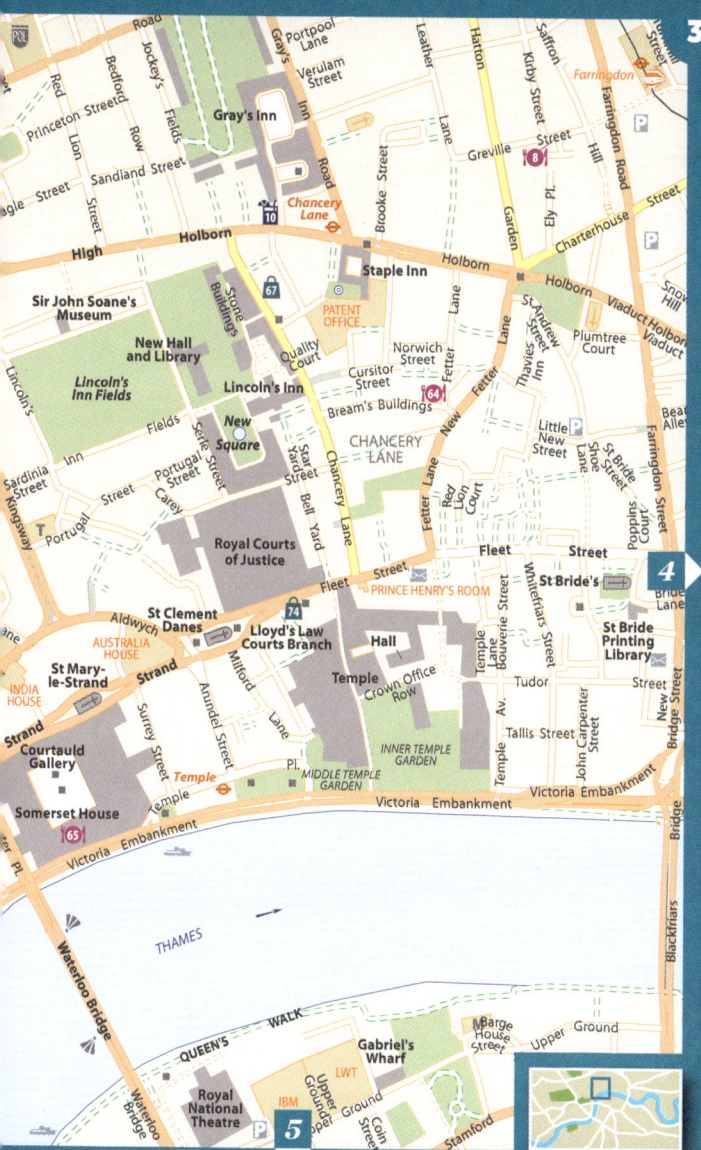

Farringdon

Portpool Lane
Jockey's Fields
Gray's Inn Road
Leather Lane
Hatton
Saffron Street
Kirby Street
Farringdon Road

Princeton Street
Bedford Row
Verulam Street
Greville Street
8
Ely Place
Charterhouse Street

Gray's Inn

Eagle Street
Red Lion Street
Sandland Street
Brooke Street

Chancery Lane
10

High   Holborn   Holborn   Holborn   Viaduct Holborn Viaduct   Snow Hill

Staple Inn

Sir John Soane's Museum
Stone Buildings
67
PATENT OFFICE

New Hall and Library
Quality Court
Norwich Street
St Andrew Street
Thavies Inn
Plumtree Court

Lincoln's Inn
Cursitor Street
Fetter Lane
Little New Street
St Bride St
Poppins Court

Lincoln's Inn Fields
Bream's Buildings
64

Lincoln's
Inn
Fields
New Square
CHANCERY LANE
New Street
Shoe Lane
Farringdon Street
Bear Alley

Sardinia Street
Portugal Street
Carey Street
Star Yard
Bell Yard
Chancery Lane
Fetter Lane
Red Lion Court

Kingsway

Royal Courts of Justice
Fleet   Street   St Bride's
4

St Clement Danes
74
Lloyd's Law Courts Branch
Fleet   Street
PRINCE HENRY'S ROOM
Whitefriars Street
St Bride Printing Library
Bride Lane

AUSTRALIA HOUSE
Hall
Temple

St Mary-le-Strand
Milford Lane
Arundel Street
Crown Office Row
Temple Lane
Bouverie Street
Tudor   Street
John Carpenter Street
New Bridge Street

INDIA HOUSE
Strand
Surrey Street
Temple
INNER TEMPLE GARDEN
Temple Av.
Tallis Street

Courtauld Gallery
Temple
MIDDLE TEMPLE GARDEN

Somerset House
65
Victoria   Embankment
Victoria   Embankment
Victoria   Embankment

Blackfriars Bridge

Victoria Embankment

THAMES

WALK

QUEEN'S   WALK   Upper   Ground

Barge House Street

Gabriel's Wharf
LWT

Royal National Theatre
IBM
Upper Ground
Colin Street
Upper   Ground
Stamford

Waterloo Bridge

5

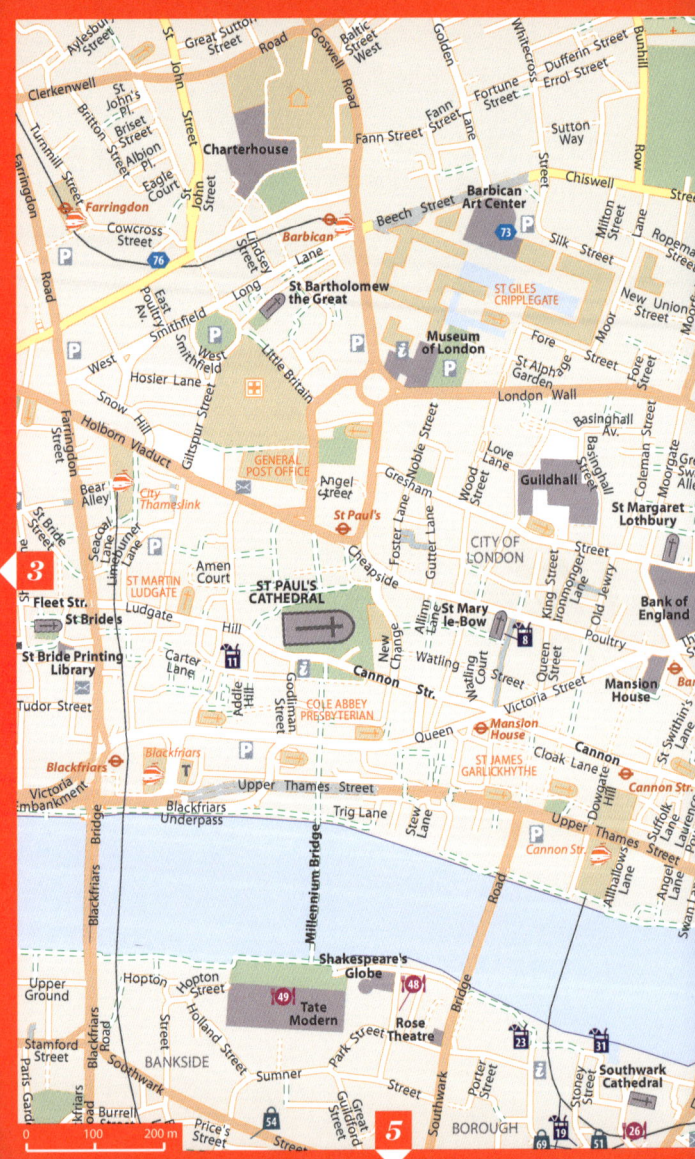

WHERE TO EAT

On **Brick Lane** (⊖ *Shoreditch*) are a number of **curry houses** ideal for eating Indian specialities on the cheap (dishes around £10). Our favourites include: **Aladin Brick Lane** 2 *(132 Brick Lane - ✆ 020 7247 8210 - www.aladinbricklane.co.uk)* and **Bengal Village** 6 *(75 Brick Lane - closed lunchtime).*

13 **Cafe Spice Namaste** - *16 Prescot St. - ⊖ Tower Hill - ✆ 020 7488 9242 - www.cafespice.co.uk - closed Sun - dishes £8-20.* You'll find all the colour and flavour of India here, as well as attentive service and a friendly atmosphere.

15 **Canteen** - *2 Crispin Pl. - ⊖ Liverpool Street, Shoreditch - ✆ 0845 686 1122 - www.canteen.co.uk - dishes £10-20.* You'll find traditional, hearty English fare here: pies, fish and chips, daily roast, sausages and mash.

38 **New Armouries Café** - *Tower of London - ⊖ Tower Hill - ✆ 020 3166 6991 - closed evenings - dishes around £10.* Housed in a room of the Tower, this small restaurant offers hot dishes, sandwiches and pastries.

TAKE A BREAK

8 **Café Below** - *St Mary-le-Bow Church, Cheapside - ⊖ Bank, Mansion House - closed evenings and weekends.* Enjoy home-made organic and vegetarian dishes in the crypt of the church or on the terrace.

11 **De Gustibus** - *53-55 Carter Lane - ⊖ St Paul's - closed evenings and weekends.* This renowned chain bakery prepares delicious sandwiches.

36 **The Ten Bells** - **PUB** - *84 Commercial St. - ⊖ Shoreditch.* This historic pub (1755) is known for being a haunt of Jack the Ripper!

Burmese cuisine in Brick Lane

Jon Arnold/hemis.fr

SHOPPING

81 **Old Spitalfields Market** - *⊖ Liverpool Street - closed Sun.* This hall hosts rotating markets (clothing, jewellery, vintage deco etc.), and its restaurants and cafés are popular with City employees at lunchtime.

72 **Petticoat Lane Market** - *⊖ Liverpool Street, Aldgate - closed Sat.* One of London's oldest street markets is a real bric-a-brac institution where you can find anything.

NIGHTLIFE

73 **Barbican Art Centre** - *Silk St. - ⊖ Barbican - www.barbican.org.uk.* This great cultural centre includes, among other things, a concert hall, a theatre and an art gallery. It's home to the London Symphony Orchestra and the BBC Symphony Orchestra.

76 **Fabric** - *77a Charterhouse St. - ⊖ Farringdon - open Fri-Sun.* Exceptional acoustics and top DJs draw a young clientele to this club.

92 **The Light** - *233 Shoreditch High St. - ⊖ Liverpool Street.* With a pleasant upper terrace, this former power station turned night club is worth visiting.

Addresses described in section 5:
26 48 49 19 23 31 51 54 69

Historic city centre turned global financial capital, the City hides among its buildings, which include major architectural achievements, from the ancient to the latest in building design.

VISIT

St Paul's Cathedral★★★ –
St Paul's - www.stpauls.co.uk - Mon-Sat 8h30-16h - £16. Built from 1675-1710, St. Paul's is Christopher Wren's masterpiece, dominating the City with its impressive scale and harmonious proportions.

Museum of London★★ – *West India Quay -*
Barbican, St Paul's - www.museumoflondon.org.uk - 10h-18h. Visit this museum for an understanding of London's historical importance across the centuries.

St Bartholomew the Great★★ –
West Smithfield - Barbican - www.greatstbarts.com - 8h30-17h (Wed-Fri 21h30, Sun 20h), Sat 10h30-16h - £4. This church is the only remaining vestige of a priory of Augustinian canons dissolved in 1539.

Guildhall★ – *Gresham St. - St Paul's*
- www.cityoflondon.gov.uk - 10h-16h30 (Oct-Apr: closed Sun). This beautiful Gothic building (15C) is both the City Hall and the seat of the Corporation of London, which is responsible for administering the district.

St Mary-le-Bow★★ – *Cheapside -*
Mansion House - www.stmarylebow.co.uk - 7h30-18h (Fri 16h) - closed Sat-Sun. The tower rising above Cheapside contains the famous Bow Bells.

Royal Exchange★ – *Corner of Threadneedle St. and Cornhill - Bank.*
The former London Stock Exchange ceased operations here in 1939. Now the neo-Classical building is occupied by restaurants and luxury shops.

Bank of England and the Royal Exchange

St Margaret Lothbury★ –
Bank - www.stml.org.uk - Mon-Fri 7h15-17h15. Inside this Wren-designed church (1686-1690) you'll find beautiful 17C woodwork★ among the best of which are the reredos, communion rails and font.

Lloyd's★★ – *1 Lime St. - Bank.* With
its stairways, lifts and façade pipes, this tower has a futuristic appearance not unlike another project its architect Richard Rogers was involved in, the Centre Pompidou in Paris.

The Gherkin – *30 St Mary Axe -*
Aldgate. Built in 2004 and designed by Norman Foster, "The Gherkin", as Londoners call it, is one of the most notable architectural achievements on the London skyline.

Monument★ – *Fish St. Hill -*
Monument - www.themonument.info - 9h30-18h (winter 17h30) - £4. This column was erected to commemorate the Great Fire that devastated London in 1666. Climb to the top (311 steps) for a view over the City.

St Mary-at-Hill★★ – *Monument -*
Mon-Fri 10h-16h. An austere façade conceals barrel vaults in a Greek cross pattern and a coffered dome.

Tower of London★★★ – *Tower Hill - www.hrp.org.uk - 9h-17h30 (Sun-Mon 10h; Mar-Oct 16h30) - £21.45.* A fortress turned prison, the Tower of London was as much a place of horror as royal pomp. Today it houses the magnificent crown jewels.